Take Your Public Speaking to the Next Level!	vii
Introduction	ix

1. CULTIVATE A SPEAKER'S MINDSET — 1

The Psychology Behind Fear: Unravel the Mindset	2
The Power of Positive Visualization Before Hitting the Stage	6
Embracing Imperfection: Accept and Grow from Your Speaking Flaws	9
Build a Growth Mindset: Lessons from Famous Speakers	11
The Importance of Resilience to Overcome Challenges	13

2. PRACTICALLY MANAGE NERVOUSNESS BEFORE YOUR EVENT — 16

Turn Anxiety into Your Ally	17
Harness Your Nervous Energy for a Dynamic Presentation	22
Use Critique Constructively to Reduce Your Anxiety	24
Transform Your Speech with Mental Rehearsal	27
Power Poses and Their Impact on Your Speaking Confidence	29
Pre-Speech Rituals Boost Your Confidence	32

3. UNDERSTANDING AND CONNECTING WITH YOUR AUDIENCE — 35

The Art of Tailoring Your Message	35
Craft Your First Five Minutes for Maximum Engagement	38
The Power of Empathy: Connect With Your Audience Emotionally	40
Engagement Strategies for Diverse Audiences	42

Adapt in Real-Time	44
Build an Emotional Connection Through Storytelling	46

4. CRAFTING IMPACTFUL CONTENT AND STORIES — 50
The Elements of a Persuasive Speech	51
Storytelling Mastery: Techniques for Memorable Speeches	53
Simplify Complex Ideas for Any Audience	56
Create Visual Aids That Enhance Your Message	58
Calls to Action: Motivate Your Audience to Move	61
What do you think of this book?	65

5. POLISH YOUR SPEAKING STYLE AND BODY LANGUAGE — 68
Find the Full Range of Your Voice	68
The Non-Verbal Toolbox: Gestures, Posture, and Movement	71
Handling Nervous Ticks and Mannerisms	73
Dress for Success: What Your Attire Communicates	75
Master the Pause: Timing for Effect	77
Use Humor Effectively Without Being a Comedian	79
Command the Stage With Your Movement	81

6. LEVERAGE TECHNOLOGY IN YOUR PRESENTATIONS — 84
Audio-Visual Aids: How to Use Them	85
The Essentials of Effective Presentation Slides	87
Amplify Your Message Pre-Event with Social Media	90
Engage Audiences with Interactive Polling Software	92
Practice Your Speech with Virtual Reality	94
Video Recording Your Speech for Self-Analysis	95
Handle Technical Difficulties Gracefully	98

PUBLIC SPEAKING MASTERY MADE SIMPLE

THE ULTIMATE GUIDE TO UNLOCK YOUR SPEAKING POTENTIAL, OVERCOME ANXIETY, AND COMMAND THE STAGE

CRISTIAN PARCO

Copyright © 2024 by Cristian Parco

All rights reserved.

No part of this book may be reproduced in any form or by any electronic or mechanical means, including information storage and retrieval systems, without written permission from the author, except for the use of brief quotations in a book review.

Contact us for any queries at:

7. REAL-WORLD APPLICATION AND
   COMMON SCENARIOS — 101
   The Art of the Impromptu Speech — 102
   Adapting Your Speech for Different Venues
   and Formats — 105
   Practical Strategies for Adapting Your Speech — 107
   Handle Difficult Questions and Interruptions
   with Ease — 110
   Refine Your Elevator Pitch — 113
   Position Yourself as a Thought Leader in Panel
   Discussions — 115

8. CONTINUOUS IMPROVEMENT AND
   ADVANCED STRATEGIES — 119
   Incorporate Feedback for Ongoing
   Improvement — 119
   Advanced Storytelling Techniques for
   Seasoned Speakers — 122
   Leverage Technology: Apps and Tools for
   Speakers — 124
   Beyond the Stage: Public Speaking for Media
   Appearances — 127
   Crafting Your Brand Through Public Speaking — 129

   Conclusion — 133
   Did you benefit from this book? — 135
   Bibliography — 137

TAKE YOUR PUBLIC SPEAKING TO THE NEXT LEVEL!

Sign up for our mailing list to receive exclusive updates, tips, and tools for mastering the stage.

We will give you access to:

- Updates on new resources and publications to enhance your speaking
- Exclusive insights and strategies not covered in the book.

🔗 **Visit** https://leadershipmastery.org.uk or scan the QR code below to unlock free resources, including:
- Speech templates
- Practice guides
- Bonus content from this book

Don't just speak—stand out. Sign up today and start your journey toward unforgettable presentations!

INTRODUCTION

Every year, millions of intelligent and highly competent individuals confront an invisible barrier that holds them back from reaching their full potential. It is not a lack of expertise nor a deficit of ambition but a crippling fear of public speaking. I remember this all too well. I was once in your shoes, with my thoughts clouded by anxiety every time I faced an audience. I would get a rapid heartbeat when a public speaking engagement came up, have sweaty palms before and during the speech, and deal with a nagging doubt that ate away at my self-confidence. My breakthrough came when I read into the notion that fears and anxieties are natural, but they can be overcome. This was the foundation for transforming my engagement with a public speaking event. *Public Speaking Mastery Made Simple* is a transformation distilled into a book so you can get over your speaking fears and anxieties and share your message with as many people as possible.

With years of experience in public speaking and countless hours spent guiding individuals through their fears of the spotlight, I've crafted a method that combines personal insights with proven strategies. *Public Speaking Mastery Made Simple* is more than just a collection of techniques; it is a transformative guide built from real-world experiences and enriched with practical exercises designed to turn theory into action.

This book is structured around a clear and powerful vision: to transform you from an anxious speaker into a confident orator. It addresses the full spectrum of public speaking, from developing the right mindset and preparing meticulously to delivering your message with impact and applying these skills in various real-world scenarios. Mastering public speaking is about refining your delivery, but more importantly, it is a journey of personal growth and empowerment.

Here is a brief overview of the five-step guideline:

1. **Develop the right mindset**

Learn to shift your perspective on public speaking and embrace it as an opportunity, as well as practical techniques to manage your anxieties. (**Chapter 1 and Chapter 2**)

2. **Prepare for your speech**

Dive into analyzing your audience, constructing your speech, and using visual aids for the greatest impact. (**Chapter 3 and Chapter 4**)

3. **Polish your delivery**

Enhance your speaking style and body language to engage and captivate your audience and command the stage. (**Chapter 5 and Chapter 6**)

4. **Apply and learn from experiences**

Practice your skills in typical speaking scenarios and learn to handle Q&As with assurance. (**Chapter 7**)

5. **Refine your skills**

Use feedback to refine your approach and elevate your public speaking skills. (**Chapter 8**)

Engage with this book actively. Treat it as a conversation between us. The exercises and reflection prompts are here to facilitate your journey, making the learning process interactive and practical. By the end of this guide, you will have learned how to speak effectively in public and gained a profound confidence that extends well beyond the podium.

Let this be your call to action. Embrace the journey with an open mind and a commitment to practice, and you will discover that the art of public speaking can open doors to personal and professional opportunities you never imagined. Together, let's break through those barriers and make your voice heard.

1
CULTIVATE A SPEAKER'S MINDSET

There are many skills that propel professionals to the peak of their careers, one of which is public speaking, which stands out as both critically important and deeply feared. It is fascinating that even seasoned leaders can experience a racing heart and trembling hands at the prospect of addressing an audience. This commonality doesn't just highlight the pervasiveness of public speaking anxiety but also sets the stage for transforming that fear into a powerful ally in your professional toolkit.

This chapter is dedicated to educating you on the biological and psychological reasons behind this anxiety so you can be well-informed and subsequently be in control rather than let your body dictate terms. I will also share the importance of cultivating the right mindset so you can make sustainable changes that will carry you through all aspects of life. By internalizing the knowledge here, you can begin a transformation where your fears and anxieties are turned into springboards for your success in public speaking and give you transferable skills to ooze confidence anywhere.

THE PSYCHOLOGY BEHIND FEAR: UNRAVEL THE MINDSET

Understand the Origins - The Fight or Flight Response

At its core, the fear of public speaking is an evolutionary response. Historically, being the center of attention was often a matter of life or death. In early human societies, standing out from the group could make one a target for predators or adversaries, leading to a deep-rooted association between visibility and vulnerability. This is often known as the fight or flight response, where in the face of danger, or even a perception of it, we react by either wanting to stand up and face the threat or flee from it. In the moment, we experience physical responses of increased heart rate, sweating, trembling, or even nausea, which can manifest as anxiety for some but the desire to face the challenge for others. While the stakes are no longer life-threatening, this primal fear persists. It manifests as anxiety when we stand before an audience due to a perceived threat to our social standing.

Understanding the biological basis of this response is crucial in facing the challenge head-on. The fight or flight response is initiated by the amygdala, the part of your brain responsible for detecting threats and activating your body's alarm system. This triggers the release of adrenaline, which prepares your body for quick action. While this response was useful for our ancestors, it can be counterproductive in modern public speaking scenarios. Luckily, there are several techniques that you can employ to calm this response. These include breathing techniques, mindfulness, and grounding. Later in this book, I will elaborate on these in a dedicated chapter on <u>Practical Strategies for Managing Nervousness</u>

Before Your Event. These are techniques I have used to great effect when they were needed. By practicing these simple techniques, you can train your mind and body to respond differently to the stress of public speaking. Over time, you'll find that your fight or flight response diminishes, making it easier to remain calm and focused.

The Spotlight Effect

Having talked about the biological causes of anxiety, it is important to know there is also a psychological aspect as well, which can trigger the biological response. Psychologists have identified the root of the anxiety as stemming from a fear of judgment from society. It is a natural reaction to the potential for negative evaluation, where your mind is preoccupied with preserving your social standing and reputation. Social psychologists call this cognitive bias the spotlight effect, which is the tendency to overestimate how much others notice and scrutinize your appearance and behavior. One study on the spotlight effect in 2000 demonstrated the extent to which some people overestimate how they are perceived in the eyes of others. In this study, college students were asked to wear an embarrassing t-shirt to class. They were then asked to estimate how many of their peers would notice it. While 50% of the students claimed their fellow students would notice, only about 25% reported noticing the shirts.

The spotlight effect often manifests in one of three things: concerns about your appearance, overemphasizing your flaws, and the possibility you might make mistakes which you will be judged and ridiculed for. To put this into perspective, think about times when you've observed others speaking. Were you critically evaluating their every word and gesture, or were you more focused on the content and how it applied to you? Did you spend the whole evening thinking about their crooked tie or the color of their shoes, or were you focused on how you resonated with the story told? By reversing the roles and understanding your audience is probably more focused on their thoughts, you can shift your mindset from fear to a more realistic view of their attention. This can motivate you to concentrate your energy on improving the quality of your content.

The Cognitive Behavioral Approach

One practical approach to managing the physical and psychological response is to engage with cognitive-behavioral strategies. They can be a powerful tool in transforming your style of public speaking. These techniques involve identifying and systematically challenging the negative thought patterns contributing to your fear. For example, if you often think, "I'm going to embarrass myself," you might replace this with, "I am well-prepared and capable of handling this speech." This method of cognitive restructuring, or changing destructive thoughts, can significantly mitigate irrational fears and build a more positive and realistic perception of your speaking abilities.

There are three elements to this:

1. **Identify** the specific thoughts that trigger your fear. Write them down and examine the evidence for and against them. Often, these fears are based on exaggerated beliefs.
2. **Replace** these negative thoughts with more balanced and constructive ones. For instance,

instead of thinking, "Everyone will judge me harshly," you could think, "Some people may judge me, but many will be supportive, and my message is more important than their opinions." This shift in perspective can help you approach public speaking with a more confident and positive mindset.
3. **Practice** positive visualization techniques. Before your speech, close your eyes and imagine yourself engaging your crowd with confidence. Visualize the audience responding positively, nodding in agreement, and applauding at the end. This mental rehearsal can create a sense of familiarity and reduce anxiety.

Neuroplasticity and Fear

Another crucial aspect in engaging the techniques and strategies in this book more effectively is understanding the brain's power. Neuroplasticity is the brain's ability to reorganize itself by forming new neural connections, which is critical to overcoming public speaking anxiety. Each time you engage in public speaking, you create and strengthen neural pathways associated with speaking confidently. Consistent practice is essential here; by facing public speaking situations, you can reduce anxiety over time.

This process is like muscle memory. Just as a musician practices an instrument to improve, you can practice public speaking to reduce fear. Each positive experience builds confidence, reshaping your brain's response to public speaking tasks. To leverage neuroplasticity, seek opportunities to speak in public, even in low-stakes environments. Join a local Toastmasters club, volunteer to lead meetings, or practice in front of friends and family. Each of these experiences helps to reinforce the neural pathways associated with confidence and competence. Additionally, review your performances with a critical eye. Focus on what went well and identify areas for improvement. This reflective practice enhances your skills and strengthens positive neural connections.

By understanding and applying these principles, you can transform your approach to public speaking from fear to opportunity. This shift enhances your ability to communicate effectively and empowers you to take on leadership roles that require strong public speaking skills. As you progress through this chapter, keep these cognitive and physiological insights in mind. They are your first tools in building a confident speaker's mindset.

THE POWER OF POSITIVE VISUALIZATION BEFORE HITTING THE STAGE

Visualization is a testament to the intricate relationship between the mind and performance, particularly in high-pressure situations like public speaking. It is a mental rehearsal technique that harnesses the brain's neuroplasticity, enabling you to psychologically prepare for public speaking engagements before stepping onto the stage. This tool is a dynamic process that enables you to visualize and internalize success. It involves creating, refining, and embodying an effective speaking scenario within your mind's confines.

What is the science behind this powerful technique? Visualization activates the same neural networks that actual physical performance does. When you vividly imagine delivering a speech, your brain generates an internal simulation of the activity, complete with emotional and physiological responses. This process is based on research that suggests mental practices can improve motivation, boost confidence and self-efficacy, alleviate stress, and enhance performance. When you visualize, you are training your brain to believe in your ability to perform tasks in ways that mirror actual achievement. For instance, athletes often use this strategy to enhance their physical performance, picturing themselves executing perfect movements. In public speaking, foreseeing a successful presentation can set the stage for the reality you aspire to create.

How can you practice visualization? First, imagine yourself delivering your speech. Run through the speech from the opening remarks to the main body of your speech and then your conclusion with a call to action. You must practice this so you feel comfortable with the content of what you will deliver and how you will transition from one phase to the next. Visualizing any humor or short stories you will incorporate in your speech is important so you can feel comfortable with them. In addition, it is important to utilize all five senses to enhance the feelings and emotions associated with public speaking to ensure the effectiveness of visualization. The value of incorporating all your senses in your visualization is understated. It brings the experience to life and allows you to feel the emotions in a way that you can anticipate the highs and lows and preempt the anxiety you may feel during the speech. The more detailed your visualization, the more vivid it feels, and the more effectively it primes your mind and body to act per this envisioned reality. I will now demonstrate the amount of detail you should build into your practice.

Picture the physical stage you will speak on. Imagine yourself walking confidently onto it, the audience's faces attentive and expectant, eagerly waiting to hear you share something with them. Smell the faint scent of the wood of the podium and the air conditioning cooling the room. See yourself opening with a short story and then delivering your opening lines with a calm demeanor, a clear and loud voice projecting to the person at the back of the room. Envision the nods of agreement or thoughtful expressions of engagement from the audience as you progress through your key points whilst hearing the slight buzz of the audience as they react to your points. Enhance this visual narrative by imagining the feel of the microphone in your hand or the clicker for your presentation slides. Finally, picture the sound of applause at the end of your talk, after your powerful conclusion and call to action.

Finally, integrating this technique into your pre-speech preparation routine can significantly enhance positive results. Make visualization a regular practice in the days leading up to your speech by dedicating a few minutes each day to review your visual success story, each time adding more detail or adjusting scenarios to suit your growing confidence better. This consistency reinforces the mental imagery and turns it into a ritual that automatically triggers a self-assured mindset as you prepare to speak.

By embracing positive visualization, you equip yourself with a tool that prepares you for successful public speaking and builds a foundation of confidence in other professional areas. This technique, based on scientific principles and practical application, provides a proactive approach to mastering the art of public speaking through mental preparation. This ensures that when the moment comes, you are ready to speak and inspire.

EMBRACING IMPERFECTION: ACCEPT AND GROW FROM YOUR SPEAKING FLAWS

In a professional working environment, perfectionism is often seen as a desirable trait, but in public speaking, it can be a barrier to excellence. The relentless pursuit of flawlessness can be paralyzing, especially when it comes to such a personal and exposed activity as public speaking. The reality is that perfection in public speaking is not just unattainable; it is also not particularly engaging. Audiences connect more deeply with authentic and human speakers—flaws included. When you embrace your imperfection, you create opportunities for genuine connections and profound learning experiences that are more impactful than flawless delivery.

Consider the common scenario where a speaker stumbles over a word or loses their place in their notes. The perfectionist might spiral into self-criticism and anxiety, further disrupting the flow of the presentation. In contrast, a speaker who has embraced imperfection might pause, smile, and acknowledge the mistake before moving on, thereby maintaining the connection with the audience. This approach not only alleviates the pressure on the speaker but also endears them to the audience, enhancing the relatability of the presentation. Embracing imperfection does not mean striving to make mistakes but accepting that errors are a natural part of the learning and speaking process. Regardless of its outcome, each speaking opportunity is a step on the steep curve of learning and personal development. Just as an experienced climber understands that every ascent improves their ability, speakers must recognize that every presentation enhances their skills and deepens their experience.

In embracing imperfection and the natural flow of public speaking, one must also learn to navigate the responses that follow each presentation. This brings us to the distinction between feedback and criticism, an essential component of the learning process. While both can be valuable, understanding the difference helps utilize each constructively. Feedback is typically specific, actionable, and objective. It focuses on the presentation and offers insights that can lead to improvement. For instance, a colleague might suggest that speaking more slowly could help clarify complex points. Or pacing left and right on stage slowly, rather than quickly, can allow the audience to focus more and not get distracted by your constant movement.

Conversely, criticism can sometimes be more general and subjective and might feel more personal. For example, it could be a comment like, "That didn't sound very confident." The key to growth is in the interpretation and use of both. Seasoned speakers listen to feedback and hone in on the constructive elements in each. They use this information to refine their skills, adjust their performances, and enhance their delivery, turning potential negatives into powerful tools for improvement. In embracing imperfection and the natural flow of public speaking, one must also learn to navigate the responses that follow each presentation.

Reflecting on the experiences of renowned public speakers can also be incredibly enlightening. Many of the most celebrated orators have faced significant setbacks and failures. Winston Churchill, for instance, was not known as a natural speaker. He struggled with a speech impediment and even experienced several public speaking failures that could have easily ended his speaking career. However, these hurdles did not deter him. Instead, they fueled his determination to master the art of oration. His persistence and willingness to learn from each setback helped him conquer challenges and cemented his status as one of history's greatest orators.

Churchill's experience underscores the transformative power of embracing imperfections and viewing each speaking opportunity as a learning experience.

In the professional world, public speaking is often a critical element of leadership and influence. Embracing imperfection is not just beneficial; it is necessary. It fosters a growth-oriented mindset that values continuous improvement over the unattainable ideal of perfection. This mindset encourages innovation, resilience, and authenticity, which are qualities that define great speakers and leaders. As you continue to develop your public speaking skills, remember that perfection is not the goal. Instead, the aim is to connect, convey, and captivate, irrespective of imperfections.

BUILD A GROWTH MINDSET: LESSONS FROM FAMOUS SPEAKERS

The maturity to embrace imperfection and take feedback constructively facilitates the development of a growth mindset. The growth mindset, popularized by psychologist Carol Dweck, refers to the belief that abilities and intelligence can be developed through dedication and hard work. In public speaking, embracing a growth mindset is crucial because it transforms challenges and failures into opportunities for enhancement and learning. This perspective is not just beneficial; it is essential for anyone who wants to excel in effectively communicating in front of an audience.

Consider the journey of some of the world's most renowned speakers with a growth mindset. For example, Winston Churchill's early career was marked not by flawless rhetoric but with persistence in the face of public speaking challenges. His early speeches in the House of Commons were often poorly received, noted more for their lack of impact than for their eloquence. However, Churchill viewed these experiences not as failures but as opportunities to refine his skills. His relentless effort to improve through practice and the study of past speeches eventually led to some of the most iconic addresses in history. One of these is his renowned "We shall fight on the beaches" speech, which not only exemplified his command of language but also his deep understanding of the power of rhetoric to inspire a nation.

Another modern example is Oprah Winfrey, who has often spoken about the role of feedback in her development as a speaker. Early in her career, she was demoted from her job as a news anchor because someone told her she was not fit for television. Instead of letting this setback define her, Oprah used it to catalyze her personal and professional development. Her ability to connect with audiences, whether on her talk show or during a commencement speech, is rooted in her belief that every interaction is an opportunity to learn and grow.

To cultivate a growth mindset in public speaking, start by setting learning rather than performance goals. In other words, focus on what you can learn from each speaking engagement, regardless of its immediate outcome. For instance, instead of striving for the perfect speech, set a goal to improve engagement with the audience or use feedback to enhance clarity. This shift in focus helps maintain motivation, reducing the fear of failure that can inhibit taking risks in your presentations. It is also beneficial to reflect on your speaking experiences and identify specific areas for improvement. After each presentation, reflect on what went well and what could be better. Did you notice the audience's interest wane at any point? Could your call to action have been more powerful? Were you able to convey your core message effectively? Reflection is a cornerstone of the growth mindset because it transforms every experience into a learning opportunity, continuously refining your skills.

Overcoming setbacks is another area where a growth mindset proves invaluable. By its nature, public speaking involves moments of uncertainty and vulnerability, which can lead to setbacks such as stumbling over words or experiencing a technical malfunction. Those with a growth mindset navigate these challenges by viewing them as temporary and surmountable. Instead of being discouraged, they analyze what went wrong, seek feedback, and develop a plan to avoid similar issues. This proactive approach helps recover from setbacks more quickly and builds resilience, ensuring that each step back is followed by two steps forward.

Embracing a growth mindset is not about ignoring your weaknesses but welcoming them as opportunities for development. It involves a commitment to continuous learning and an openness to feedback, both critical for public and professional communication success. By adopting this mindset, you improve your public speaking skills and enhance your capacity to lead, inspire, and make a lasting impact on your audience. Every speech, feedback session, and moment of reflection takes you one step closer to becoming a better speaker and a profound communicator who can genuinely make a difference.

THE IMPORTANCE OF RESILIENCE TO OVERCOME CHALLENGES

In public speaking, resilience is the capacity to persistently face and overcome the challenges and setbacks inherent in mastering this crucial skill. In being resilient, you can bounce back from a poor performance or a tough crowd, but more importantly, you continually push forward and hone your ability to communicate effectively even when progress feels elusive. This ability to adapt and thrive in speaking challenges is invaluable, particularly in high-stakes environments where every word can influence decisions and perceptions.

Several methods can be used to build resilience in public speaking, including exposure therapy, a technique borrowed from clinical psychology but equally applicable in this context. Exposure therapy involves gradually and repeatedly exposing yourself to the source of your fear—in this case, public speaking. Start with a low-stress situation, such as speaking in front of a mirror or recording yourself on camera, then gradually increase the stakes. Move on to speaking in front of a small, supportive group. Then, perhaps, consider a community group or a professional seminar. Each exposure provides an opportunity to face your fears, learn from the experience, and build confidence. This methodical escalation helps you to desensitize to the anxiety associated with public speaking, turning fear into the ability to conquer the challenge.

In addition to exposure therapy, try positive affirmations to build resilience. These are positive, empowering statements you repeat to yourself to foster self-belief and overcome the cycle of negative thoughts. For instance, before a presentation, you might tell yourself, "I am well-prepared, and my message is important," or "I am a confident and capable speaker." These affirmations can teach your brain to associate public speaking with positive self-beliefs rather than negative fear-based narratives. Over time, this practice boosts your confidence and fortifies the mental resilience needed to tackle public speaking challenges effectively.

Another mechanism to develop resilience is cultivating a supportive network. This could be through a mentor who provides guidance, a coach who offers professional improvement tips, or even colleagues who encourage you. A supportive environment provides emotional encouragement and enriches learning with diverse perspectives and constructive feedback. This network is especially valuable during setbacks as it provides an external viewpoint and the reassurance needed to persevere.

Just as in many areas of professional and personal development, resilience in public speaking is both a shield and a catalyst. It shields you from the discouragement that can accompany setbacks while simultaneously catalyzing growth by encouraging a persistent, proactive approach to overcoming obstacles. By actively building and nurturing resilience, you equip yourself with a vital tool for public speaking and any professional challenge. This turns potential setbacks into stepping stones for success. True resilience in public speaking means viewing each speaking opportunity as a chance to learn and improve, ensuring that every word is heard and resonates, leaving a lasting impact on your audience.

2

PRACTICALLY MANAGE NERVOUSNESS BEFORE YOUR EVENT

In professional settings, every speech can significantly impact careers and corporate directions, meaning that if you struggle with pre-speech anxiety, managing it is not just beneficial—it is imperative. It is vital to understand how to transform nervous energy into a positive force that can set the stage for delivering powerful presentations and fostering a persona of confidence and authority. This chapter explores two practical strategies to help you before and after your speaking engagement to conquer your nervousness. You will understand the transformative power of visualization and mindfulness—techniques that have gained recognition for their effectiveness in reducing stress and their ability to enhance focus and presence in high-pressure environments. Another highlight of this chapter is understanding how personalized rituals can help you bring your anxiety under control and finally demonstrate the importance of interpreting feedback with a positive mindset, so it is an opportunity for growth rather than a trigger to reinforce your anxieties. I have tried to maintain a systematic approach in this chapter by exploring mindset strategies first and strategies that are more biological in nature second.

TURN ANXIETY INTO YOUR ALLY

Mindfulness Explained

Mindfulness is a modern therapeutic practice that refers to the psychological process of bringing your attention to the present moment without judgment. When you practice mindfulness, you engage in a form of mental training that cultivates a heightened awareness of the here and now. This focus on the current moment helps break the cycle of worry that can overwhelm you before you make a public appearance. Instead of being trapped by fears of future mishaps or dwelling on past speaking blunders, mindfulness roots you in the present, where such anxieties lose their grip. It is relatively simple as a practical exercise. Still, it requires consistent practice over some time for it to be effective in reducing anxiety levels before a speaking engagement. Aside from this, studies have shown that mindfulness can aid a higher quality of sleep, better emotional regulation, and give you clarity of thought to assist you in making better choices. There are several techniques—some of which I will explain below—you can employ to become more mindful. These exercises can be used in your daily life as well as before going on stage.

Outside of speaking engagements

1. **Eat, walk, and drive mindfully**

We perform many daily activities that often become

mundane and feel like we are just going through the motions. The root cause is that we have become desensitized and oblivious to the sensory input, cognitive processes, and physical benefits of performing those actions. If this has become you, then the power to change is in your hands. It is as simple as focusing on the textures of the foods, taking a moment to smell the food you are about to eat, or clearing your thoughts while you walk around the block. All it requires is for you to block out intrusive thoughts and focus on the activity at hand. At first, you may struggle to keep that focus for more than a few seconds. With consistent practice, you will be able to hold that focus and enjoy the activity, but more importantly, have clarity of thought and teach your mind not to be desensitized and just go through the motions simply because it is overstimulated or overwhelmed. In the long term, this will be extremely important for being able to control any anxiety associated with a public speaking engagement. Remember that it is most effective when you practice this in short bursts consistently, rather than long sessions infrequently.

2. **Meditation practices for speakers**

Meditation is another technique that offers a structured method for deepening your capacity to control focus and alleviate stress. Tailored meditation practices for speakers can involve guided imagery, where you visualize a successful speaking engagement in vivid detail, as discussed in the previous chapter. Alternatively, focused attention meditation, where you concentrate on a single reference point—such as your breathing, a specific object, or a word or phrase—can significantly enhance your mental discipline. Engaging in these practices regularly, especially in the days leading up to a public speaking event, can train your brain to default to a state of calmness and presence when you most need it. If you anticipate a struggle to meditate alone, you should consider group meditation sessions. These sessions often provide a supportive environment where individuals can explore mindfulness and meditation under the guidance of an instructor. The group's collective energy can also enhance your individual experience, giving a sense of shared objectives and mutual support in managing anxiety.

Furthermore, including mindfulness and meditation in your pre-speech routine offers benefits beyond reducing nervousness. These practices foster a broader resilience to stress, enhancing overall well-being and performance in various aspects of life, including high-stakes business environments. By incorporating these practices into your preparation, you may discover that not only does your fear of public speaking decrease, but your overall stress levels will reduce, leading to improved concentration, better decision-making, and increased professional efficacy. In essence, mindfulness and meditation equip you with the tools to survive and thrive in the demanding world of business leadership and public communication.

3. **Visualization**

Earlier in Chapter 1.2 I highlighted the role of visualization in overcoming your fears of public speaking in general, irrespective of if you have been invited for a speech or not. In this segment I want to highlight that even seasoned speakers can experience anxiety prior to speaking engagements, which is why they also continually engage with visualization so they can remain in control and not be paralysed by anxieties. As a reminder, the key elements of an effective visualization are to make them as detailed; make them vivid and real by utilising as many of your senses as possible; practice it in advance of your speaking engagement.

For Instant calm before getting on stage

1. **Present moment focus**

A fundamental part of reducing pre-speech anxiety through mindfulness involves being able to focus your attention on the present moment. Techniques to achieve this focus include mindful breathing and sensory awareness exercises. A simple yet effective practice is the '5-4-3-2-1' technique, where you pause and use your senses to notice five things you can see, four you can feel, three you can hear, two you can smell, and one you can taste. This exercise does not require any unique setting or preparation, making it an ideal tool for moments when pre-speech anxiety begins to surface. Focusing on your senses helps to shift your mind away from anxious thoughts about your upcoming speech. It reconnects with the present environment, which calms your mind and equips you with a clearer, more focused mental state. All it requires is for you to concentrate on your breathing and experience your environment through your senses.

2. **Breathing Techniques for Instant Calm Before Speaking**

In public speaking, where nerves can be as much a part of the experience as the audience, understanding the physiological impact of your breathing is crucial. Your breath bridges the mind and body, directly influencing the nervous system. When you engage in controlled breathing, you tap into the body's natural ability to regulate stress responses. Slow and deep breathing activates the parasympathetic nervous system —often called the "rest and digest" system—which calms the body and reduces anxiety. This physiological shift is crucial for alleviating immediate symptoms of stress and maintaining composure and control as you step onto the stage.

Let's explore specific breathing techniques that can be used before and during your public speaking engagements to effectively manage nervousness. One powerful method is the "4-7-8" breathing technique, which involves breathing in for four seconds, holding the breath for seven seconds, and exhaling slowly for eight seconds. This technique helps regulate the heart rate and focuses your mind, diverting it from the cycle of anxious thoughts that can occur before a presentation. Another technique is diaphragmatic breathing, or "belly breathing," which focuses on expanding the diaphragm rather than the chest during breathing. This method increases oxygen intake and triggers body relaxation responses, making it particularly useful before you take the stage.

Incorporating these breathing exercises into your pre-speaking routine can significantly enhance their effectiveness. Consider setting aside specific times during your preparation to practice these techniques, such as at the beginning of your day or right before you rehearse your speech. Remember to practice consistently. Doing so not only makes these techniques more effective in reducing anxiety but also makes them more intuitive to use under stress. It is also helpful to combine breathing exercises with other pre-speech preparations—like reviewing notes or setting up presentation materials. This integration creates a holistic routine where each element supports and enhances the other, leading to a more composed and confident presentation style. Over time, this practice can help you manage your immediate nervousness and bring a newfound confidence and feeling of being able to conquer any task thrown at you with public speaking no longer being the dark shadow in your closet.

As you continue to explore and apply these breathing strategies, remember that the goal is to make them a seamless part of your public speaking toolkit. With regular practice, controlled breathing can become a reflexive response to public speaking anxiety. This will enable you to handle even the most daunting speaking engagements calmly and confidently. Once you have refined this skill, it will extend beyond the podium, enhancing your ability to manage stress and maintain composure in various professional situations, reinforcing your effectiveness as a leader and communicator.

HARNESS YOUR NERVOUS ENERGY FOR A DYNAMIC PRESENTATION

When you step onto the stage, the surge of adrenaline and the accompanying flutter of nerves is a natural, albeit often unwelcome, part of public speaking. Traditionally, we view nervous energy as an obstacle to a successful presentation. However, when reframed and managed correctly, this same energy can become a powerful ally, transforming a potentially flat delivery into a dynamic and engaging performance. Recognizing nervous energy as a vital force rather than a deterrent is the first step in this transformation. When channelled effectively, this energy can enhance your enthusiasm and presence, making your speech more compelling.

The process of reframing nervous energy begins with a shift in perspective. Instead of perceiving this energy as a sign of impending failure, interpret it as a precursor to excitement and heightened alertness—states that can significantly enhance your performance. This shift is rooted in the understanding that the physiological responses to excitement and anxiety are remarkably similar. Interpreting these responses as so dictates whether they will benefit or hinder you. By welcoming nervous energy as a natural enhancer of your presentation, you prepare your mind to leverage it as a tool for improvement rather than a barrier to success.

Once you've reframed your view of nervous energy, the next step is to learn how to channel this energy into your delivery effectively. Techniques for this include focusing on the passion behind your message and using movement to dissipate excess energy. Passion is a powerful motivator and can convert nervous energy into expressive and persuasive communication. Before your presentation, spend a few moments reconnecting with the core reasons behind your speech. Why is this message important to you? How does it resonate with your values or excite you? This connection can transform anxiety into enthusiasm, naturally engaging and captivating the audience.

Additionally, physical movement can be an excellent conduit for nervous energy. Instead of standing rigidly at a podium, allow yourself to move around the stage. Use gestures to emphasize points and to keep your body engaged. This movement helps manage physical manifestations of nervousness—like shaking hands or a trembling voice—and projects confidence while keeping the audience's interest. However, it is crucial to balance this movement with purpose. Aimless pacing can be distracting. Instead, use deliberate and controlled movements to reinforce your message, such as walking towards the audience during crucial points to create a sense of closeness and immediacy.

Maintaining control over your nervous energy is essential to ensure it enhances rather than overwhelms your presentation. Strategies to maintain this control include regular practice and focusing on the rhythm of your speech. Frequently rehearsing under conditions like those you will face during the actual presentation can help you get used to the emotional and physical sensations you will experience which will make it easier for you to manage them effectively during the actual presentation. Additionally, it is important to pay attention to the pace of your delivery. Nervous energy can cause you to speed through your presentation, so consciously slow down your speech, allow pauses for emphasis, and allow your points to resonate with the audience. These pauses will enable you to collect your thoughts, take a breath, and give your audience time to absorb and reflect on what you have said.

As you integrate these strategies into your public speaking practice, remember the goal is to transform your relationship with nervous energy. Embrace it as a part of your speaking dynamics, channel it to emphasize your passion, and control it through deliberate practice and presentation techniques. This approach will improve your delivery and change your entire public speaking experience, making it more vibrant and effective. By mastering the art of harnessing nervous energy, you equip yourself with a powerful tool that ensures your presentations are successful and memorable.

USE CRITIQUE CONSTRUCTIVELY TO REDUCE YOUR ANXIETY

Every presentation can shape how people see you and open new doors, which means it is important to solicit feedback and learn from it because it is essential for growing and mastering your skills. Building a solid feedback loop with your audience or practice groups is key to becoming a better speaker. Simply put, a feedback loop is a way to receive, understand, and use the information from your performance, to turn raw comments into valuable insights that you can act on.

To initiate a constructive feedback loop, start by identifying who will provide you with feedback will be. These could be colleagues, mentors, or even members of your audience who have witnessed your presentations. Once identified, encourage open and honest feedback by asking specific questions about your speaking style, content clarity, and audience engagement. You can facilitate this through digital means like surveys or feedback forms or more directly through post-presentation discussions. It is crucial to approach this phase openly and clearly understand that the primary goal is to improve, not validate.

The next step is interpreting feedback as constructive, which is essential to leveraging it effectively. At first, this is difficult because it involves separating personal feelings from the critique received. Feeling defensive or disheartened when faced with criticism is natural however, it is important to shift your mindset to view feedback as a valuable tool for learning rather than a personal indictment. Focus on the specifics of the feedback rather than the way it is said. Categorize it into themes: for example, many noted your strengths in engaging the audience, but felt your slides were overly complex. Others found your ability to project your voice was good, but were distracted by your movements. Such categorization helps pinpoint areas for improvement without getting overwhelmed by the volume of data.

Finally, acting on feedback is where the real transformation happens. Begin by prioritizing the input based on what can significantly impact your speaking. For instance, if there is a consensus that your speaking pace is too fast, consider this a key area for immediate adjustment. Implement small changes in manageable steps to ensure you can thoroughly evaluate each modification for effectiveness. Practice with a metronome or record your practice sessions to monitor and adjust your speed for the pacing issue. After making adjustments, seek more feedback to assess if the changes were effective or need further tweaking. This iterative process not only improves your current skills but also encourages a habit of continuous learning and adaptability.

The long-term benefits of a well-structured feedback loop extend far beyond incremental improvements in specific presentations. Regularly engaging in this cycle can significantly boost your confidence as a speaker. With each piece of feedback that you apply to your public speaking, you enhance your skills and gain a deeper understanding of your unique strengths and weaknesses. This knowledge empowers you to tailor your public speaking approaches to better meet your audience's needs, thereby increasing your effectiveness and impact as a communicator. Additionally, the ongoing nature of this process promotes a mindset of continual improvement, which is invaluable in keeping your skills relevant and sharp in an ever-evolving professional environment.

Furthermore, the skills you develop when receiving and acting on feedback have broader professional benefits that can be transferred to leadership, team management, and interpersonal communications, which are areas where mechanisms for external input are integral to success. Thus, mastering the art of the feedback loop can enhance your communication and professional capabilities, making you a more effective leader who can direct and guide a team to a vision with greater mastery and confidence.

TRANSFORM YOUR SPEECH WITH MENTAL REHEARSAL

Earlier in the book I mentioned the role and importance of visualization in being able to build the right mindset for public speaking. The focus of that discussion was in being able to overcome your fears before even accepting a public speaking engagement. In this chapter, I want to focus on the fact that you have already accepted the engagement and need to be mentally and physically prepared for it. As a strategic tool, the principles are the same, where you picture the scene and deliver a speech. However, the fundamental difference is that now the speech is real, not hypothetical, meaning that you have already prepared a speech for an engagement and are going on stage in a few hours.

This technique is a strategic tool that empowers you to visualize and mentally experience a successful presentation before it happens and involves running through your speech, visualizing the content and the delivery in as much detail as possible. The benefits of preparing this way include enhancing familiarity with the material, bolstering confidence by mentally simulating successful outcomes, and further reducing anxiety levels.

The most effective mental rehearsals follow the following steps:

i. Find a quiet, undisturbed space to focus without interruptions.
ii. Close your eyes and take deep breaths to center your thoughts.
iii. Picture the venue of your presentation — see the stage, the audience, and the lighting.

iv. Methodically walk through your speech from start to finish, from your opening lines to the final question and answer from the audience

This technique is different from visualization in terms of the objective, which is to rehearse the specific content you will deliver, rather than overcome specific fears regarding speaking in front of people. Although you will get a secondary benefit of reducing stress levels, it is not the primary focus, so if your mind is trying to focus on the emotions surrounding public speaking, you should try to divert your attention from that and focus on the content of the speech itself. As with visualization, if you make this rehearsal vivid and detailed, it will yield better results by making you more confident in whatever message you want to share with your audience, and subsequently allow you to direct energy during your presentation to deal with unexpected situations.

By combining mental rehearsal with physical practice, you can dramatically improve your overall preparation. After completing your mental run-through, engage in the physical practice of your speech. This could include standing up and delivering your speech aloud in an environment like the one you will be in during the event. The transition from mental to physical rehearsal helps to integrate the cognitive and physical aspects of your speech delivery, making your preparation more comprehensive. Alternating between psychological and physical rehearsals in your practice sessions is beneficial, ensuring that both your mind and body are equally prepared for the demands of public speaking.

As we close this chapter on managing nervousness before speaking, it is important to recognize that preparation is essential. From mindfulness and breathing techniques to the strategic use of mental rehearsal, each method offers unique benefits that can transform your approach to public speaking. These strategies prepare you to handle the nerves associated with speaking and empower you to deliver presentations with confidence and authority. The next chapter will build on these foundations, focusing on techniques for engaging your audience—an essential skill for turning your well-prepared speech into a memorable and impactful communication experience.

POWER POSES AND THEIR IMPACT ON YOUR SPEAKING CONFIDENCE

In public speaking, your body language is silent but speaks volumes at the same time. It is an essential component of communication and is profoundly influential in shaping the self-perception and the audience's receptivity of the message. Before delving into the specifics of power poses, it is crucial to understand that your posture and gestures can either amplify your confidence or betray your anxieties. Strong and open body language fortifies your self-assurance and enhances your credibility and engagement with the audience when aligned with your verbal message. Conversely, closed or defensive body language can create a barrier, subtly signalling discomfort or insecurity, which may cause the audience to question the authenticity or reliability of your message.

The concept of power posing involves adopting postures historically associated with dominance and authority. These poses are typically expansive, involving open limbs and an upright stance, occupying space and projecting confidence and control. The psychological benefits of engaging in power poses stem from their impact on personal hormone levels. Specifically, they can increase testosterone - associated with confidence and assertiveness - and decrease cortisol - associated with stress and anxiety. This hormonal shift can significantly influence your sense of empowerment and readiness, making power poses a valuable tool. It is important to remember that a power pose is not intended to convey arrogance and does not make you overconfident, rather it is intended to boost your self-belief and project confidence to your audience, demonstrating that you are in control and have mastery over what you are saying.

In practice, you should start integrating them into your pre-speaking routine for two minutes at a time in front of a mirror, which is often enough to begin feeling the effects. Below are some examples of power poses you can incorporate into a routine and then try on stage or when delivering a lecture or speech in front of a smaller crowd in a conference room.

The Wonder Woman or Superhero

Stand tall with your feet shoulder-width apart, place your hands firmly on your hips, and lift your chin slightly. Visualize yourself as a superhero, ready to tackle any obstacle that comes your way.

The Victory

Stand upright with your feet slightly wider than hip-width apart. Raise your arms above your head in a V-shape, with your palms facing outward. This stance exudes triumph and confidence.

The CEO

Sit or stand with your legs crossed and interlace your

hands behind your head. Lean back slightly while maintaining an open and relaxed posture. This pose communicates authority and leadership.

The Open-Arms

Stand or sit with your arms extended wide to the sides. Lift your chest and hold your head high. This position signifies openness, approachability, and self-assuredness.

The Warrior

Stand with your feet wide apart, one foot ahead of the other. Firmly plant your back foot on the ground and bend your front knee, lowering your body into a lunge. Raise your arms above your head, stretching them wide. This stance represents strength, determination, and resilience.

Remember that these poses are not just physical exercises, but are also mental preparation for the attitude you want to embody. Practice these in the privacy of a meeting room or even a restroom before you go on stage. Consistency and context are key; regularly practising these poses in situations that mimic the speaking environment can condition your mind to trigger confidence when you most need it.

As you explore these strategies, remember that the goal is to align your body language with the message you wish to convey. Power poses can help to recalibrate your physical presence to one that supports your speaking objectives, enabling you to occupy the stage not just physically but with conviction and authority. By mastering this aspect of non-verbal communication, you fortify your public speaking repertoire, ensuring that before you even speak, your body has already begun to communicate your strength and confidence to the audience. Over time, this practice will enhance your performance in individual speaking engagements and contribute to a more enduring sense of self-assurance in your professional interactions.

PRE-SPEECH RITUALS BOOST YOUR CONFIDENCE

Rituals play a significant role in shaping our everyday lives. They provide structure, help us reduce anxiety, and mentally prepare us for the challenges ahead. In public speaking, a pre-speech ritual can be particularly beneficial. It serves as a psychological cue that signals your brain that it is time to perform. This cue helps shift your mindset from preparation to execution, reducing anxiety by fostering a sense of familiarity and control in an otherwise unpredictable situation. In other words, rituals anchor you in the present and redirect your focus from anxiety to the task at hand.

When creating a personal pre-speech ritual, it is crucial to consider what resonates with you. A ritual that works well for one speaker might not work for another. The goal is to find actions that calm your nerves and boost your confidence. For some, this might involve a series of physical warm-ups or vocal exercises. For others, it could be a quiet moment of reflection or reviewing critical points of the speech. The first step in creating this ritual is to clearly understand what triggers your anxiety, and identify the strategies that have historically helped you manage these feelings. Begin by listing activities that help you relax or bring you joy, then consider how to incorporate them into a short routine before each speaking engagement.

For example, a successful entrepreneur who is known for

his captivating speeches starts his ritual with ten minutes of solitude spent in a quiet corner of the venue, practising deep breathing and visualizing the successful delivery of his speech. He then listens to an energizing song to set a positive tone for his performance. Another example involves a renowned keynote speaker who recites a personal mantra that reaffirms her capabilities and value to her audience. She pairs this with a series of stretches that relax her muscles and helps to alleviate physical manifestations of stress.

These examples show that effective rituals are often simple but deeply personal. They don't have to involve elaborate preparations; instead, they should focus on key actions that trigger a mental shift from anxiety to confidence. When designing your ritual, start small. Choose one or two activities that you know have a positive impact on your mindset and then build from there. Consistency is critical—perform your ritual before every speech, no matter the size or significance of the event. This consistency helps to reinforce the ritual as a trigger for your performance mindset.

As you gain more experience and confidence in public speaking, your pre-speaking ritual may need to change. What worked for you at the beginning of your career might not be as effective as you gain more experience and confidence. It is important to regularly reflect on the effectiveness of your ritual and make adjustments when necessary. Perhaps the solitude that once calmed you now makes you feel isolated, or the physical exercises that used to energize you now feel redundant. Be open to these changes and willing to experiment with new components to keep the ritual aligned with your current needs and circumstances.

Adaptability also applies to different speaking contexts. A ritual that works for a small, intimate workshop might not be suitable for a large, formal conference. Consider the environment and audience of each speaking event and tweak your ritual accordingly. For example, you could consider spending a few minutes networking with the audience before a community talk to build rapport or taking some time alone to review your slides before a high-stakes corporate presentation. The goal is to ensure that your ritual remains a relevant and effective tool for boosting your confidence and performance.

Incorporating these practices into your pre-speech preparations is important. Remember that the ultimate purpose of your ritual is to ensure that you are in the best possible mental state for speaking. It should provide you with strength and assurance, and become a personal tradition you look forward to as part of your speaking engagements. As you hone your public speaking skills, allow your ritual to evolve, serving as a faithful companion on your path to becoming a more confident and effective speaker.

3
UNDERSTANDING AND CONNECTING WITH YOUR AUDIENCE

A public speaking engagement can be considered a dance in which the audience is your partner. Their reactions, engagement, and feedback play pivotal roles in shaping the success of your presentation. Understanding and connecting with your audience isn't just about adjusting your speech to suit their tastes—it is about resonating with them on a deeper level, creating a symphony of interaction where each word you speak and each response you elicit are harmonious. This chapter delves into the art of audience analysis to enable you to tailor your message with precision and care, ensuring that your words reach your listeners and motivate them. In the appendix of this book, there is a practical step-by-step guide on how to analyze your audience. You can reuse this guide, speech after speech, until it becomes second nature to you.

THE ART OF TAILORING YOUR MESSAGE

Identify Audience Needs and Preferences

Understanding your audience is the initial step in connecting with them. This involves understanding their demographics, such as age, profession, cultural background, and interests, as well as delving deeper into their needs, preferences, and challenges they face, that your speech can address.

Creating audience personas can be incredibly useful in this situation. It involves constructing detailed profiles of typical audience members. For instance, if you are speaking at a technology conference, you might have personas such as the tech startup CEO looking for new strategies or the software developer seeking more profound knowledge in a specialized field. These personas help you anticipate the questions they might have, the problems they need solving, and the aspirations they hold. This insight allows you to tailor your speech to feel personal and relevant to each listener.

Customize Content and Delivery

Once you understand the needs and preferences of your audience, the next step is to customize your content and delivery to suit them. This customization involves more than just choosing the right words—it is about adjusting the tone, structure, and even the visual aids you use to make them appropriate for the needs and expectations of your target demographic.

For instance, if you speak to a group of industry experts, your presentation will probably be packed with technical details and industry jargon. However, if your audience is composed of novices, the same approach might overwhelm and alienate them. Instead, you can use more straightforward language, provide basic explanations, and share engaging stories to explain complex concepts in relatable manner. Similarly, a younger, more dynamic audience might appreciate a fast-paced presentation with visual aids and interactive elements, while a more traditional business audience might value a slower, more deliberate pace with detailed data charts.

Language that Resonates Not Alienates

The language you use in your presentation can significantly impact how well your message is received. Choosing words and phrases that resonate with your audience helps you retain their attention and build rapport, whilst using language that mirrors the vernacular of your audience increases your relatability and credibility.

For example, using precise, data-driven language can help establish your expertise and credibility when addressing a group of finance industry professionals. Conversely, if you are speaking to a community group about health and wellness, a more conversational tone using everyday language and personal anecdotes may be more effective.

Use Pre-Speech Surveys

One practical method to ensure your speech meets the expectations of your audience is to conduct pre-speech surveys. These surveys can ask questions about what your audience hopes to learn, the issues they consider most important, and how they prefer to receive information. The insights gathered from these surveys can be invaluable in fine-tuning your content and approach.

For instance, before a digital marketing workshop, a quick survey could reveal that the majority of participants need help with using social media for business. With this insight, you can adjust your presentation to focus more heavily on this aspect, directly addressing the immediate needs of the participants. This will make your workshop more relevant and valuable.

Incorporating these strategies into your preparation process transforms your approach to public speaking from a one-size-fits-all delivery to a tailored, impactful experience. By taking the time to understand and connect with your audience, you can enhance the effectiveness of your communication and simultaneously forge deeper connections that can lead to lasting impressions and relationships. As we explore other facets of audience engagement in this chapter, remember that the foundation of any successful speech is a deep, empathetic understanding of those you are addressing. This understanding is what allows you to communicate and resonate.

CRAFT YOUR FIRST FIVE MINUTES FOR MAXIMUM ENGAGEMENT

The opening moments of your presentation have a big impact. During this time, your audience forms their first (and often long-lasting) impression, deciding whether to lend their full attention or retreat to the recesses of their phones and thoughts. This critical window is your opportunity to capture and, more importantly, hold their interest. By setting a compelling tone right from the start, you create a pathway for a successful interaction that resonates with and captivates your audience throughout your presentation.

The first few minutes act as the gateway to your speech and should not only introduce the topic but also ignite curiosity and interest. Consider what your audience will find intriguing, surprising, or immediately relevant to craft your opening. This could be an unexpected statistic that challenges common perceptions, a provocative question that prompts introspection, or a brief story that humanizes your topic. For example, if your speech is about the importance of cybersecurity, beginning with a recent, relatable incident involving a well-known company can immediately draw your audience's attention by highlighting the relevance and immediacy of the issue. By using hooks and questions effectively you will get your audience to think actively instead of just passively consuming information. A question, especially one that poses a moral or strategic dilemma, can be particularly effective as well. It encourages the audience to project themselves into your scenario, making the discussion personal and engaging. For instance, asking, "What would you do if you knew your personal data was being sold?" will actively engage the audience and make the discussion more personal. This technique will keep the audience engaged and prepare them for the depth and nature of the exploration to follow.

Building rapport quickly within the first few minutes is crucial and can be achieved by demonstrating empathy and authority. Show that you understand the audience's challenges and goals and clearly articulate how your presentation will address these. This alignment reassures the audience that your speech is worth their time and attention. Techniques such as mirroring the audience's language and referencing shared experiences or common goals can establish a connection quickly. For example, if addressing a group of entrepreneurs, mentioning your own experiences or challenges in starting a business can create an immediate sense of camaraderie and trust.

Furthermore, the tone you set in these initial moments lays the groundwork for the interaction that follows. Remember to use a tone that balances professionalism with approachability. This will make the audience feel respected, comfortable, and open to receiving and interacting with your message. Adjusting your vocal delivery to suit the content and context is important. You might start with a softer, more reflective tone if sharing a personal anecdote or a more vigorous, assertive tone if presenting a call to action. This helps modulate the audience's emotional response to suit your objectives.

By meticulously planning the opening of your speech and integrating these strategic elements, you ensure that you capture and retain the audience's attention throughout your presentation. This will improve the effectiveness of your communication and strengthen your connection with the audience, fostering a dynamic and interactive speaking environment. As you continue to refine your public speaking skills, remember that the success of your presentation often depends on the strength of its opening. A well-crafted beginning sets the stage, pace, and tone for all that follows, establishing a framework within which your message can be effectively received and appreciated.

THE POWER OF EMPATHY: CONNECT WITH YOUR AUDIENCE EMOTIONALLY

Empathy, often revered as the backbone of effective communication, plays a pivotal role in public speaking. When you as a speaker can genuinely understand and empathize with your audience, you bridge the gap between mere presentation and meaningful connection. This empathetic connection not only improves receptivity but also deepens engagement, making your message more persuasive and memorable. To cultivate this connection, you must first immerse yourself in the emotional and intellectual dimension of your audience, understanding their desires, fears, and expectations with as much clarity as yours.

Developing empathy in public speaking begins with active listening and involves going beyond just the words said by your audience, extending to the interpretation of the emotions of your listeners. This requires paying close attention to what is said during interactions like Q&A sessions and informal discussions, as well as to what remains unspoken. Non-verbal cues such as body language, facial expressions, and even silence, can provide insights into the mindset and emotional state of your audience. For instance, a speaker addressing a new policy change might notice a cross-section of the audience looking particularly tense or concerned. By acknowledging these non-verbal signals and addressing the concerns directly, the speaker demonstrates empathy and care for the audience's feelings, thus enhancing the trust and connection within the room.

In addition, empathy involves anticipating and addressing any potential concerns or objections regarding your topic. This proactive approach shows you understand and respect alternative perspectives. It also helps keep your presentation flowing smoothly by preventing potential disruptions that might arise from unaddressed concerns. For example, suppose you are presenting a new technological tool to a group of seasoned employees accustomed to traditional methods. They may be skeptical about the necessity and utility of the new system. By acknowledging these potential concerns at the beginning of your talk and providing clear, evidence-based benefits of the latest technology, you can alleviate apprehensions and encourage a more open reception to the information you share.

Incorporating empathy into your public speaking engagements transforms the dynamic of speaker versus listener into a collaborative exchange. It shifts the focus from simply delivering content to creating a shared experience where the audience feels seen, heard, and valued. This elevates the impact of your message and fosters a deeper connection with your audience, paving the way for more effective and impactful communication. As you refine your public speaking skills, remember that empathy is not just a tool for enhancing presentations; it is a vital component of all successful interpersonal interactions, enriching both the speaker and the audience.

ENGAGEMENT STRATEGIES FOR DIVERSE AUDIENCES

In the dynamic world of public speaking, engaging a diverse audience can often feel like navigating a complex maze with multiple potential paths, each leading to different outcomes. Whether you're addressing a room of seasoned professionals or a mixed group with varying levels of understanding and interest, the key lies in employing a range of interactive techniques that cater specifically to the diversity of your audience. Interactive methods such as Q&A sessions, live polls, and group discussions can transform a conventional presentation into a vibrant, interactive dialogue, encouraging participation and making the experience more memorable for everyone involved.

Q&A sessions, for instance, serve as a direct bridge between you and your audience, allowing for real-time engagement and clarification. When you open the floor to questions, you allow your audience to seek clarification on points of interest and raise concerns or viewpoints you might have yet to consider. This can enrich the content of your presentation and demonstrate your respect for the audience's input. This can increase their engagement and investment in the topic. Live polls are another powerful tool, especially in larger settings where individual voices might otherwise remain unheard. By integrating real-time polling into your presentation, you can gather instant feedback or gauge opinions. This can then steer the direction of your talk, making it more aligned with the audience's interests and concerns.

Group discussions can be particularly effective in workshops or smaller group settings where interaction is more manageable. Breaking the audience into smaller groups and assigning specific topics based on the segments of your presentation encourages peer-to-peer interactions. This makes the learning experience more engaging and allows diverse perspectives to surface, enriching the broader discussion and deepening the audience's understanding of the subject matter.

Incorporating visual and multimedia elements into your presentations is another strategy to ensure the content resonates with a diverse audience. People have different learning styles—some are visual learners, while others may prefer auditory or textual information. By combining text, images, videos, and infographics, you can cater to these varied preferences, making your presentation more accessible and engaging. Take infographics, for instance. When discussing complex data or trends, a well-designed infographic can convey your message more effectively than a list of statistics. Similarly, videos can breathe life into stories and testimonials, providing a real-world connection to the discussed concepts that text alone may not fully deliver.

Personal anecdotes and stories are invaluable for creating relatable and engaging content. Sharing personal experiences or relevant stories can help break down the formal barrier between you and the audience, making you more approachable and your message more relatable. Sharing from your life humanizes you and illustrates your points in a way that is easier for the audience to understand and remember. Each story you tell can act as a hook, drawing your audience in and helping them connect the dots in a way that abstract concepts or raw data cannot.

Implementing feedback mechanisms is crucial in understanding and enhancing audience engagement. You can gather feedback through digital forms at the end of your session or by asking the audience to rate their understanding or interest at various points during the presentation. This immediate feedback can be incredibly insightful, helping you adjust your pace, focus on topics that need clarity, or modify your delivery style to better meet the audience's needs. For example, if feedback indicates the audience is struggling with a particular concept, you can revisit it with additional examples or simplify the explanation. This ensures your audience keeps up and demonstrates your commitment to their learning and engagement, fostering a more interactive and responsive speaking environment.

In integrating these diverse strategies, you aim to create a presentation that informs, resonates, and engages. By understanding your audience and employing a mix of interactive techniques, visual aids, personal stories, and feedback mechanisms, you can enhance the effectiveness of your communication. This approach not only makes your presentations more engaging but also more memorable, ensuring that your message reaches and inspires your audience. Engaging effectively across different audiences remains a crucial hallmark of successful public speaking, whether speaking to a boardroom of executives or a community hall filled with residents.

ADAPT IN REAL-TIME

In public speaking, the ability to read and respond to your audience's non-verbal cues is as crucial as the content of your speech. These cues, including body language, facial expressions, and the room's general atmosphere, can offer valuable insights into your message's receptivity. Mastering the art of interpreting these signals is not just about enhancing your sensitivity as a speaker; it is about actively engaging in a dialogue with your audience, even if they are not speaking.

Nonverbal communication is often the most telling feedback you can receive during a presentation. For instance, you might notice a participant's furrowed brows and crossed arms as a sign of confusion or disagreement. Conversely, you may see another participant leaning forward, nodding, and smiling, signalling interest and agreement. These cues can guide you in real-time, allowing you to adjust your pace, clarify points that might not have landed as intended, or even alter the trajectory of your presentation to better align with the audience's mood and reactions. It is essential to maintain flexibility in your presentations to accommodate these shifts, ensuring that your message reaches your audience and resonates with them on a deeper level.

Adjusting on the fly is a skill that comes with practice and the presence of mind. It requires you to remain fully engaged with your material and audience, ready to shift gears at a moment's notice. For example, if you detect signs of waning interest during your session—perhaps through side conversations, smartphone usage, or general inattentiveness—you can introduce an interactive element, such as a quick poll or a direct question to the audience. This tactic can recapture their attention and bring focus back to your presentation. Similarly, if you perceive skepticism or confusion about a particular point, it might be wise to pause and invite questions or provide additional examples to clarify your message. By doing this, you can ensure your audience is on the same page as you and demonstrate your commitment to their understanding and engagement.

Real-time problem-solving is another critical aspect of adapting during presentations. Despite meticulous planning, unexpected challenges can arise, such as technological failures, interruptions, or unforeseen audience reactions. Handling these situations with composure and decisiveness is pivotal. If, for example, your slideshow fails, having a backup plan in place, such as printed copies of your slides or a whiteboard ready to use, can save you from losing the professional edge. Similarly, if an audience member interrupts with a challenging question or comment, responding patiently and tactfully will help maintain a constructive atmosphere. Always acknowledge the comment or question; if it is not the right time to address it thoroughly, assure the attendee that you will revisit it later in your presentation or discuss it privately afterwards.

These strategies for reading and responding to audience cues in real-time enhance the effectiveness of your communication and build trust and credibility with your audience. They know you are not just there to speak but to engage in a meaningful exchange—a conversation that respects and values their input and adjusts to meet their needs and expectations. As you continue to hone these skills, you'll notice that your ability to connect with and impact your audience will grow, making every presentation a performance and a dialogue that enriches you and your listeners.

BUILD AN EMOTIONAL CONNECTION THROUGH STORYTELLING

There are many techniques to build an emotional connection with an audience, from music to visual effects, to carefully selecting the clothes you wear when you speak. However, storytelling is one such technique that has a profound impact and extends beyond simply sharing events—it is a powerful vehicle for human connection, breaking down barriers and fostering a deep, emotional bond between speaker and audience. Understanding the psychological underpinnings of storytelling reveals that stories engage more parts of the brain than factual data. When you hear a story, it activates the language-processing parts of your brain as well as the areas used for experiencing sensations and emotions. This dual activation allows the audience to live through the events of the story, making the experience and its message more memorable and impactful. Further in the book I will elaborate on the specifics of weaving stories into your speech and share some of the types of stories to utilize, however, in this chapter I want to share some of the psychology behind stories and why they are so effective. Jump to the chapter on storytelling here.

Crafting a compelling story requires more than an exciting narrative. It demands an understanding of the key elements that make stories resonate. The structure of a good story typically involves setting the scene, introducing a conflict or challenge, building tension through rising action, climaxing with a main event, and then resolving the narrative. Each element intends to pulls the audience deeper into the world you are creating.

Take, for example, the story of a young entrepreneur facing seemingly insurmountable challenges in launching her startup. By detailing her initial struggles, the pivotal moments of crisis, and her eventual triumph, you keep the audience engaged and highlight the resilience and determination needed to succeed in the business world. The key is to weave your factual message—perhaps the importance of perseverance and innovation in entrepreneurship—into the emotional fabric of the story, making the lesson both digestible and impactful.

Authenticity and vulnerability are critical in storytelling, especially when the goal is to connect with your audience. Sharing your failures, doubts, and fears serves can humanize you and validate the experiences and emotions of your audience. It creates a shared space of mutual understanding and respect where your audience can feel safe as they reflect on their journeys and challenges. For instance, if a CEO shares personal stories of early career mistakes and the lessons learned, fostering a culture of openness and continuous learning within the company. This vulnerability can significantly enhance connection with the audience, making the messages about learning from mistakes and embracing growth more relatable and convincing.

There are some stories which are etched in everyone's mind because those successful speakers have used storytelling to great effect. For example, TED Talks that captivate millions, often start with the speaker drawing the audience into their journey of discovery and transformation. They open with stories that start with a personal anecdote introducing the speakers' challenges and the emotional stakes, followed by how their experiences led to a broader insight or solution. The personalized nature of the story makes the speaker's conclusions feel more credible and relatable, effectively transforming the audience's perspective on the topic. It is important to remember that storytelling is more than conveying information. It is about creating a relatable experience that transports the audience, evokes emotions, and fosters a profound connection. The stories you choose to share and how you tell them can powerfully influence how your message is received and remembered. Whether you are addressing a conference room or a crowded auditorium, the ability to craft and deliver stories that resonate can transform your public speaking from ordinary to extraordinary.

As we transition from understanding and connecting with your audience to mastering the delivery of your speech, the techniques and insights from this chapter provide a strong basis for engaging your audience in more meaningful and impactful ways. The next chapter will build on this, refining your presentation skills to ensure that your voice, rhythm, and body language align perfectly with the powerful stories and connections you've established. This holistic approach to public speaking ensures clarity and coherence in your presentations and a lasting impact beyond the final applause.

4
CRAFTING IMPACTFUL CONTENT AND STORIES

Imagine standing before a crowd, the energy palpable, every pair of eyes on you, waiting for your words not just to inform but to move them, change their perspectives, and ignite action. This is the essence of a genuinely impactful speech. It is not merely the words you choose, but how you weave them into a powerful narrative that captivates and compels. In this chapter, I will delve into the architecture of persuasion, discovering how to construct speeches that transcend the mundane and resonate deeply with your audience, leaving a lasting imprint on their minds and hearts. I will share how to structure your speech to be persuasive, the method of incorporating stories into your speech to deliver your message effectively, and the importance of simplifying complex ideas so your audience stays engaged while understanding key pieces of information. Finally, I will share how you can use visual aids effectively to enhance and not distract from your message.

THE ELEMENTS OF A PERSUASIVE SPEECH

1. The Structure

A persuasive speech is a skillful combination of well-structured elements to guide the audience from curiosity to conviction. At its core, a compelling speech consists of an introduction, body, and conclusion, each serving a distinct purpose yet contributing to the speech's overall goal. Your introduction should hook your listener in by presenting a stimulating question or a startling fact. The body of your speech should develop your argument with supporting evidence and persuasive rhetoric. Finally, the conclusion reinforces your message and encourages the audience to consider a new perspective or action.

2. The Thesis Statement

The foundation of your speech lies in your thesis statement. A thesis statement is the central message of your speech that concisely captures the essence of your argument. Crafting a compelling thesis requires clarity and precision—it should be specific enough to give clear direction to your speech and broad enough to encompass your main points. Think of your thesis as the backbone of your presentation, supporting and connecting all the elements of your speech. For example, suppose your goal is to persuade your company to adopt a new environmental policy. Your thesis might be, "Implementing a green workspace not only significantly reduces our carbon footprint but also enhances employee productivity and company image."

3. **The Rule of Three**

Dividing your content into three main points is a classic technique in speech-making known as the Rule of Three. This structure relies on the principle that people remember information more effectively when presented in threes. Structuring your argument around three clear, interconnected points can enhance understanding and retention among your audience. For example, if your speech is about the benefits of digital marketing, you might organize it around three key benefits: cost-effectiveness, enhanced targeting, and measurable results. This approach makes your argument more digestible and persuasive, as the grouped points create a rhythmic reinforcement of your message.

4. **The Logical Structure and Flow**

The flow of your speech is crucial in maintaining the audience's engagement and ensuring the clarity of your message. Each segment of your speech should logically lead to the next, with clear transitions that guide the audience through your narrative. Consider using signposts—phrases like "firstly," "in addition," or "consequently"—which help signal shifts in your argument or introduce new points. This logical progression ensures your audience can follow and absorb the content effectively without getting lost in disjointed arguments or unrelated details.

5. **Using Evidence Effectively**

In any persuasive speech, evidence is the bedrock of credibility. It supports your main argument and demonstrates an in-depth understanding and dedication to the topic. However, effective use of evidence goes beyond simply stating facts. It involves integrating this data into your narrative naturally to enhance your argument. For example, if discussing the impact of climate change, rather than merely citing statistics about rising sea levels, you could relate these figures to potential flooding risks in the geographical areas the audience are from, making the data more relatable and impactful. Always source your evidence from reputable, up-to-date sources, and present it in a way that supports your main argument, rather than overshadowing it.

By mastering the basic elements of crafting a persuasive speech, you equip yourself with the tools to inform, inspire, and persuade your audience. As you apply these techniques to your speech preparations, remember that the ultimate goal is to create a narrative that resonates, persuades, and remains memorable long after you have left the stage.

STORYTELLING MASTERY: TECHNIQUES FOR MEMORABLE SPEECHES

In the previous chapter I briefly touched on some of the psychological aspects of how storytelling can be powerful. In this chapter, I want to take you through some basic techniques for building a story that will make you and your message stand out and be memorable.

Incorporating storytelling into your public speaking within a business, leadership, or other professional context is not merely for artistic purposes, or to draw attention to yourself, it is a strategic tool for communication. The power of a well-told story lies in its ability to engage the audience on an emotional level, making the message heard and felt. Various techniques can elevate your storytelling, ensuring your narrative captures attention and reinforces your message with conviction. First, consider the structure of your stories. Like a great movie or novel, your story should have a clear beginning, middle, and end. The beginning sets the stage, introducing characters and settings, but more importantly, establishing the stakes: what is at risk and what you will gain. It is where you hook your audience, often with a conflict or a question that begs resolution. The middle of the story is where the action escalates; it is your opportunity to build tension and deepen the emotional investment of your audience. This part of the story often involves challenges or hurdles that the protagonist—perhaps a client or a version of yourself—must overcome, providing ample opportunity to demonstrate resilience or the effectiveness of a product or strategy.

As you approach the end of your story, it is important to focus on the resolution and reflection. Here, we draw the lessons and connect the story to your overarching message. It is crucial at this stage to make sure that the solution gives a satisfying conclusion to the narrative, answering any initial questions and resolving any conflicts that were introduced. Effective storytelling follows this arc, but it is important to tailor the complexity and depth of your story to fit the time available and how interested your audience is in the details. Too complex, and you risk losing their attention; too simple, and the story may need to engage more deeply.

Integrating humor into can enhance a story's relatability and memorability. However, it is important to approach humor sensitively and understand your audience's culture and expectations. Humor can lighten the mood and make your message more approachable, but it can also alienate or offend if used inappropriately. When incorporating humor, tie it closely to the content of your story. For example, self-deprecating humor can humanize you to your audience, making you more relatable and breaking down barriers of hierarchy or authority. The key is to keep the humor relevant and in service of the larger message, ensuring it adds value to the story rather than distracting from it.

Another pivotal aspect of storytelling in public speaking is making your stories relatable to your audience. In Chapter 3 you learnt about understanding the demographics, experiences, and the values of your target audience, now weave these elements into your narratives. Use scenarios that mirror the challenges or aspirations of your listeners and include characters they can identify with or aspire to emulate. The more your audience can see themselves in your stories, the deeper the emotional and intellectual engagement. Techniques such as vivid descriptions, relatable emotions, and specific, concrete details can bring a story to life, making the abstract concrete and the impersonal personal.

Finally, contrasting personal stories with universal parables can meet diverse audience needs and expectations, offering multiple pathways for engagement. Personal stories draw on your own experiences, providing authenticity and credibility. They allow you to share lessons from your life, making the insights you offer personal. On the other hand, the use of parables (which are often more generic and symbolic) can illustrate moral or ethical lessons. They allow audiences to abstract the lesson from the narrative, applying it to their context. Deciding when to use personal stories or parables largely depends on your audience and objectives. Personal stories are particularly effective in small, intimate settings where the goal is to build personal connections or when you need to establish your credibility or expertise. Parables work well when addressing larger audiences or more diverse groups where a direct personal story might resonate less universally.

Mastering these storytelling techniques ensures that your speeches are heard and remembered. It allows you to transform your public speaking engagements into powerful tools for persuasion and connection through the strategic use of structure, humor, relatability, and the careful selection of personal anecdotes, rather than universal narratives. As you refine your storytelling skills, remember that each story you tell is an opportunity to inform, inspire, and influence your audience in profound and lasting ways.

SIMPLIFY COMPLEX IDEAS FOR ANY AUDIENCE

When you address an audience, whether seasoned industry professionals or newcomers eager to learn, the clarity with which you present complex ideas can significantly impact the effectiveness of your communication. It is important to break down intricate concepts into simpler, digestible parts. To achieve this, identify the core components of the complex idea you wish to convey. Divide these components into manageable sections, each representing a fundamental aspect of the overall concept.

For example, if you are explaining a complex business model, you might break it down into its revenue streams, market analysis, and operational strategy. By dissecting the model into these fundamental parts, you allow your audience to grasp each segment fully before moving on to how these parts interconnect to form the larger structure.

Layering information further aids in building understanding without overwhelming the listener. Begin with a broad overview of the topic, then gradually introduce more detailed aspects as the speech progresses. From general to specific, this layering method helps anchor your audience's understanding of each new piece of information back to something they have already grasped. For instance, when discussing a new technology, start with its purpose and basic functionality before delving into the technical aspects of its operation. Each layer should serve as a stepping stone that prepares the audience for the next, more detailed piece of information, ensuring that by the end of your presentation, even the most complex ideas have been made accessible.

Using analogies and metaphors is particularly powerful in translating complex ideas into relatable terms. These rhetorical tools allow you to draw parallels between a difficult concept and something familiar to the audience, facilitating understanding through association. For example, if explaining blockchain technology, you might compare the blockchain to a ledger in a long-running family business. This analogy helps simplify the technology, making the concept of distributed and secure digital record-keeping easier to comprehend. It is important to select comparisons that relate to your audience's experiences and cultural background to ensure that the analogy improves understanding rather than causing confusion.

Avoiding or carefully explaining jargon is critical in ensuring your speech is accessible. Every industry has its terminology, but excessive jargon can alienate listeners and obscure the clarity of your message. When using technical terms, immediately follow them with a definition or explanation given in plain language. This not only aids in understanding but also boosts the audience's confidence in their grasp of the subject matter. For instance, when talking about financial instruments, don't just mention "derivative" and continue. Take a moment to explain that a derivative is a financial security whose value depends on, or is derived from, an underlying asset or group of assets. This brief pause to clarify can significantly affect how well your audience follows the rest of the discussion.

Visual aids can be invaluable in simplifying complex information. Well-designed charts, graphs, and diagrams can illustrate relationships and processes more clearly than words alone. When using visual aids, ensure they are not cluttered and that each element is necessary for understanding. Each visual should have a clear purpose, whether to highlight trends, show relationships, or depict a process flow. For example, a flowchart can represent the steps in a manufacturing process, providing a visual representation that helps the audience quickly grasp the order and method of operations. The key is to integrate these visuals seamlessly into your presentation, using them to reinforce your verbal explanations, not replace them.

By implementing these strategies, you can turn potential confusion into clarity and engagement. Breaking down complex ideas, layering information, using analogies, avoiding jargon, and employing visual aids are all techniques that, when used thoughtfully, can significantly enhance the accessibility and impact of your presentations. As you continue to develop your skills in simplifying complex information, remember that the goal is to bring your audience along on a clear, understandable path through your content, leaving them with both knowledge and the confidence that comes from truly understanding what they have learned.

CREATE VISUAL AIDS THAT ENHANCE YOUR MESSAGE

For effective communication, visual aids are not just supplementary; they are integral tools that, when used wisely, can significantly enhance the impact of your presentation. However, the key to effectively leveraging visual aids lies in adhering to fundamental design principles that ensure these aids support rather than overshadow your message. When creating visual aids, simplicity is paramount. This doesn't mean your visuals should be bare, but rather that they should be free of unnecessary clutter that could distract from the key points you are conveying. Use clean lines, ample white space, and legible fonts. Each visual element, whether a graph, chart, or image, should have a clear purpose and directly relate to the segment of the speech it accompanies.

Colors are crucial in visual prompts as they can attract attention and influence the audience's mood. It is important to pick a color scheme that reflects the tone of your message; cool blues and greens for presentations of a calm and serious nature, bright reds and oranges for energetic, compelling talks. Consistency in color usage helps maintain a coherent visual flow throughout your presentation. Similarly, the choice of typography should enhance readability and emphasis. Standardize font size, type, and color for body text, headings, and subheadings to ensure they are easy to read, even from the back of the room.

When deciding on the type of visual aid to use, consider the nature of the information you present and your audience's preferences. Graphs and charts are excellent for depicting trends, comparisons, and statistical data, making complex data more accessible and understandable. Diagrams help show processes or relationships between different elements effectively. Photographs and videos can be powerful in humanizing your story or illustrating real-world applications of abstract concepts.

Integrating visuals seamlessly into your presentation requires careful planning and consideration of timing, so you should introduce visuals at points in your speech that naturally call for a more profound illustration or reinforcement of the point you are discussing. Introduce each visual aid deliberately, allowing the audience time to absorb the information it presents before moving on. This might mean pausing after revealing a graph or inviting the audience to reflect on an impactful image. Such pauses allow comprehension and enhance retention of the information presented.

Remember to avoid common pitfalls associated with visual aids to ensure they serve as enhancements rather than distractions. A common mistake is to overload visuals with too much information; when you crowd visuals, they can overwhelm the audience, making it difficult for them to focus on the key points. Keep text on slides to a minimum, using bullet points or short, concise statements.

Another frequent issue is using visuals that do not align with the spoken content. Make sure that every visual element directly supports or adds to your message; discrepancies can confuse the audience and detract from your message. In addition, be wary of relying too heavily on your visual aids. They should supplement your speech, not replace it. Your presence, voice, and delivery are a key focal point of your presentation, and visuals should enhance your connection with the audience, not overshadow it. Be prepared to speak freely and engagingly, with visuals as backdrops to reinforce and amplify your narrative. This approach ensures that your audience remains focused on you as the speaker, with visual aids enhancing their understanding and retention of your message rather than diverting their attention.

By adhering to these principles and strategies, you can effectively integrate visual aids into your presentations. This ensures they contribute positively to the communication of your message. When used thoughtfully, these tools can transform a good presentation into an exceptional one, making your message more visually appealing, memorable, and impactful. As you continue to refine your skills in using visual aids, always consider their role in the broader context of your presentation goals, ensuring they add value and clarity for your audience.

CALLS TO ACTION: MOTIVATE YOUR AUDIENCE TO MOVE

In a well-delivered speech, the call to action (CTA) is the climax of the symphony. It is the moment when the energy of your words culminates into a clear, compelling directive that prompts your audience to move, think, or change. Understanding the importance of a strong call to action is crucial because it shifts your audience from passive listeners to active participants. It is the bridge between your ideas and the impact they can have in the real world. A potent CTA goes beyond mere suggestion; it resonates with the core motivations of your audience, tapping into their desires and challenges, and offers a clear, actionable path that aligns with the solutions or insights you have just presented.

Effective calls to action require precision and a deep understanding of your audience's needs and aspirations. You can tailor each CTA to fit the context of your speech and the specific outcomes you wish to achieve. Start by being exceptionally clear about what you want your audience to do. Ambiguity is the enemy of action. Whether you encourage them to adopt a new business strategy, change a personal habit, or support a cause, your directive should be unmistakable and imbued with a sense of urgency. For example, instead of vaguely suggesting, "Consider using renewable energy sources," a compelling CTA would be, "Start reducing your carbon footprint today by signing up for renewable energy services – here's how."

Moreover, your call to action should spark motivation. This is where understanding the triggers of your audience – their fears, hopes, and dreams – becomes invaluable. Frame your CTA in a way that emotionally connects with your listeners, perhaps by highlighting the benefits they stand to gain or the disasters they might avoid. Use strong, action-oriented verbs and paint a vivid picture of the positive outcomes of taking action. For instance, if your goal is to motivate a corporate team to pursue more significant innovation, your CTA might be, "Start by dedicating 10% of your workweek to brainstorming creative solutions to our client's most pressing issues, and witness your projects transforming from ordinary to extraordinary."

Analyzing successful calls to action can provide valuable insights into crafting your own. Consider a renowned keynote speech encouraging entrepreneurs to persist in their ventures. The speaker concluded with a powerful CTA: "Tonight, write down the one step you've been postponing in your entrepreneurial journey and commit to completing it this week. Let's turn our potential into progress!" This CTA is compelling because it is specific, time-bound, and directly linked to the entrepreneurial spirit of the audience, which values action and results.

Testing and refining your call to action is an ongoing process. Start by testing out your CTA in smaller settings, or with a segment of your target audience to gather feedback. Pay attention to how the audience reacts. Are they enthusiastic and ready to act, or do they seem confused and hesitant? Use surveys or direct feedback to understand their responses and adjust your wording or approach accordingly. Sometimes, even minor tweaks in phrasing or presentation can significantly increase a CTA's impact.

As you integrate these strategies into your speeches, keep in mind that your call to action is not just a closing statement. Rather, it is a powerful tool that can stimulate change and inspire your audience to act. By crafting clear, compelling, and actionable CTAs, you ensure that your message not only resonates in the moment, but also leads to meaningful action long after the applause has faded.

The CTA is fundamental in transforming the energy of your speech into a pathway for change. It captures the essence of your message and directs it towards specific action, ensuring that your words catalyze personal and professional transformation. As we move forward, the principles of effective CTAs conclude our discussions on creating impactful content and sets the stage for exploring the nuances of polished delivery and presentation dynamics, essential components in the skill of persuasive speaking.

WHAT DO YOU THINK OF THIS BOOK?

"The only reason to give a speech is to change the world."

— JOHN F KENNEDY

There was a time when you might have been paralyzed by fear of public speaking, or you struggled with confidence, not knowing whether you were doing the right things when you got up to speak in front of a crowd. You sought guidance, advice, and reassurance, like many others will do. Then you came across my guide, and I hope you benefitted from it. You now have an opportunity to be selfless and help those people who are struggling.

To make that happen, I have a small favor to ask…

Whether we like it or not, the reality is that people judge a book by its cover (and its reviews). So, on behalf of a public speaker on a mission to make public speaking accessible to everyone, please help fellow public speakers by leaving this book a review. It will go a long way to giving this book exposure to as many people as possible, but also help me get closer to accomplishing my mission.

If you gained valuable insights from this book, consider your review a gift. It won't cost any money, will feed into the circle of kindness, and takes less than 60 seconds. You might change a fellow public speaker's life forever and help…

- One more person overcome their fears of public speaking
- One more person deliver life changing speeches with confidence
- One more person feel empowered to share their unique message
- One more entrepreneur support their family.
- One more dream come true.

To get that 'feel good' feeling and make a difference, all you need to do is…

<u>Scan the QR code below to leave your review:</u>

I'm even more excited to help you become a confident and expert public speaker FASTER than you can possibly imagine. You'll love the lessons and strategies I'll share in the coming chapters.

Thank you from the bottom of my heart. Now, back to polishing your delivery and developing your skills further.

Your fellow public speaker,
☺

5
POLISH YOUR SPEAKING STYLE AND BODY LANGUAGE

Imagine the impact of a well-tuned orchestra; each instrument finely adjusted to play its part, contributing to a harmonious and powerful performance. Now, picture yourself as the conductor of such an orchestra. In this scenario, your instruments are the elements of your voice and body language in public speaking. Mastering these elements allows you to deliver your message with clarity and a compelling force that deeply moves your audience. This chapter delves into the nuances of vocal variety and body language. These are crucial tools that, when finely tuned, can transform your presentations from monotonous monologues into dynamic dialogues.

FIND THE FULL RANGE OF YOUR VOICE

Vocal Dynamics and Emotional Resonance

Your voice is a powerful tool. It can whisper secrets, command attention, and convey a spectrum of emotions. By mastering vocal dynamics such as pitch, pace, and volume, you can add color and depth to your speech, making your message more engaging and easier to listen to. Analyzing how these tools were employed in famous speeches can effectively show us the importance of mastering these tools. Consider Martin Luther King Jr.'s "I Have a Dream" speech, where his varied pace, strategic pauses, and changes in volume and pitch not only captured the attention of his audience but also amplified the emotional power of his message.

The pitch - the highness or lowness - of your voice helps to identify critical points or when a question is being asked. Varied pitch helps maintain listener interest and prevents your speech from sounding monotonous. The pace – speed – at which you speak is equally important. A faster pace can convey excitement or urgency, while speaking slower might emphasize a point or allow for reflection. Balancing these speeds according to the nature of your message can significantly enhance understanding and retention. It is also important to modulate your volume carefully: speaking too loudly can be overwhelming while speaking too softly can cause the audience to lose interest. Adjusting the volume to suit the room's size and the content's nature can help maintain an optimal level of engagement.

Another important tool you have in your arsenal is the tone of your voice. Aligning it with the emotional content of your message will help build an emotional connection with your audience, making your speech heard and felt. For instance, a warm and sincere tone when sharing personal stories can make your audience empathize with your experiences. Conversely, a confident, assertive tone might be appropriate when making a call to action or presenting a strong opinion. Matching your tone to your message enhances the emotional impact and reinforces your authenticity and credibility as a speaker.

Practice, Practice, Practice

Mastering the full range of your voice will take time and will only happen with regular practice. There will be some aspects that already come naturally to you, such as being able to control the pace you speak, but you may need to work on changing the pitch and tone to suit the needs of the speech. Alternatively, you may be able to project your voice exceptionally well but speak too fast. Identifying your strengths and weaknesses is the ideal starting point to build from. Alternatively, you can ask your friends and family for specific feedback regarding your voice or watch a recording of yourself and note these specific elements. While this may seem a mammoth task, it is important to break it down into manageable chunks, deal with them individually, and then begin with exercises that focus on one aspect at a time.

To improve your control of pitch, try reading a passage and intentionally altering your pitch on different words to see how it changes the impact of the message. It will seem unnatural and forced at first, but that is normal because you are intentionally trying to change a habit. However, with perseverance, you will internalize this skill and notice how natural it becomes. To work on the pace of your voice, practice delivering a segment of your speech at various speeds, noting how it affects the perception of the audience. Try this in smaller settings with friends and family or at home at the dinner table, and then work up to larger audiences. You can practice volume control by giving a speech to different-sized rooms or even recording yourself to hear how the volume changes the clarity and impact of your message.

Incorporating these vocal techniques into your speaking style isn't just about manipulating sound; it is about enriching the way you connect with your audience, ensuring your message isn't just delivered but deeply felt. As you continue to explore and practice these techniques, remember that your voice is as much an instrument as that of a musician, and with careful tuning, it can transform speeches into symphonies of communication.

THE NON-VERBAL TOOLBOX: GESTURES, POSTURE, AND MOVEMENT

Non-verbal communication is often considered a pillar of communication because its subtleties can sometimes speak louder than words. Gestures, posture, and strategic movement are indispensable tools in your non-verbal toolbox, each playing a pivotal role in how your message is received and perceived. Effective gestures can significantly reinforce your spoken words, making your message more memorable and engaging. For example, an open palm suggests honesty and openness, while a pointed finger can emphasize a key point. When used judiciously, these gestures can help punctuate your message and draw the attention of the audience to important points while simultaneously aiding in their retention of information.

However, you must maintain a harmonious relationship between body language and speech, since this can be the difference between emphasizing your message and distracting from it. To integrate these movements effectively, they should be purposeful and timed to coincide with key moments in your speech. For instance, enumerating points using your fingers can help the audience track your argument. At the same time, a well-timed gesture toward a presentation slide can make the connection between your spoken and visual content more explicit. Try to practice this in front of a mirror or record your presentation to see how your gestures appear to an audience and adjust them to ensure they add the intended value to your words.

Posture is equally critical in non-verbal communication because it shows confidence and authority. An upright posture, with your shoulders back and your head held high, projects confidence and can make you appear more convincing to your audience. In contrast, slouching or leaning heavily on a podium might suggest uncertainty or disinterest. Dynamic posture, where you maintain an upright but relaxed stance, allows for occasional shifts in position that can convey engagement and energy. This affects how the audience perceives you and can influence your confidence and assertiveness.

Purposeful movement across the stage can further enhance your engagement with the audience. Instead of standing statically at a podium, moving towards the audience during critical points in your presentation can create a sense of connection and intimacy. However, like gestures, movement should be purposeful and not distract from the message. Mapping out key spots to pause for emphasis or to engage different sections of the audience can make your movement across the stage feel more natural and impactful. This technique helps maintain audience interest and emphasizes the structure of your speech, as moving from one physical position to another can symbolize a transition from one topic to the next.

While mastering non-verbal communication can significantly enhance your public speaking prowess, you must be aware of common pitfalls. For example, a mismatch between verbal and non-verbal cues can confuse the audience or undermine the message. For instance, smiling while delivering serious or sad news can send mixed signals. Another common error is the overuse of gestures or excessive pacing on stage, which can appear nervous or unprofessional. Being conscious of these pitfalls and observing their impact through practice and feedback can help you refine your non-verbal communication skills. By developing a keen awareness of how your gestures, posture, and movement can align with your verbal message, you enhance your ability to communicate effectively and memorably. This alignment strengthens your delivery and deepens the audience's engagement with your message, making your presentations heard, felt, and remembered. As you continue to integrate these non-verbal tools into your speaking engagements, remember that they are not just embellishments to your speech but essential components that reflect your confidence, credibility, and charisma.

HANDLING NERVOUS TICKS AND MANNERISMS

When it comes to public speaking, what you say and how you say it counts. Nervous ticks and mannerisms, although common, can distract your audience, diluting the potency of your message. The first step to managing these is to recognize them. Start by recording your practice sessions, looking for repetitive movements such as fidgeting, playing with a pen, or swaying back and forth. These are often subconscious actions that manifest when we feel anxious or uncomfortable. Observing yourself through video can show you what your audience sees, helping you understand which habits need addressing.

Once identified, the next step involves tackling the root cause—being nervous. Techniques such as mindfulness can play a crucial role here. In Chapter 2, I elaborated on mindfulness, a method that involves staying present and fully engaging with the current moment without judgment. By incorporating mindfulness into your preparation, you can train your mind to focus on the message rather than the anxiety. When practised regularly before a presentation, you can calm your nerves and reduce the occurrence of nervous ticks. One particularly useful method for nervous ticks is a deep breathing technique where you inhale slowly for four counts, hold your breath for seven counts, and exhale for eight counts. This exercise will help center your thoughts and control your heart rate, making you feel more at ease.

In addition to mindfulness, thorough preparation significantly alleviates anxiety. Being well-prepared boosts your confidence and reduces the fear of the unknown—one of the primary triggers of nervousness in public speaking. This preparation involves knowing your material inside and out, and practicing your delivery multiple times to familiarize yourself with your content and how you will transition from one point to the next. This allows you to focus more on delivery and engagement with the audience rather than just recalling information.

Regular practice combined with constructive feedback is vital in refining your presentation style. One useful method I used was to participate in public speaking groups or workshops where I would present in front of an audience that provided honest feedback. There was no personal attachment to this group, from their side or mine, and we were all aware of why we were there: to help each other excel in public speaking. The feedback was invaluable as it allowed for an external perspective and helped me identify issues I might not have noticed otherwise. It also enabled me to gauge the effectiveness of the changes I was implementing. Each session allowed me to test new techniques in controlling my mannerisms, gradually helping me replace them with gestures that were harmonious with my message and enhanced it.

Remember, the goal is not to eliminate your mannerisms entirely, but to ensure they do not distract from your message. Public speaking is as much about conveying your personality as it is about delivering content. Authenticity connects, so while you aim to polish your delivery, ensure that the essence of 'you' remains intact. This balance will resonate most with your audience, making your presentations effective and memorable. Keep practicing and refining. Over time, you will find that what once made you nervous now makes you thrive.

DRESS FOR SUCCESS: WHAT YOUR ATTIRE COMMUNICATES

When you step into the spotlight, before you even utter a single word, your attire speaks volumes. The choices you make about what to wear can significantly influence your first impression on your audience, setting the tone for your presentation and impacting your credibility. This isn't just about looking good; it is about building an image that aligns with your message and resonates with your audience. The proper attire is a visual endorsement of your professionalism and authority, helping to establish trust and respect from the moment you come into view. For instance, wearing a well-tailored suit to a business presentation can project competence and seriousness. At the same time, smart-casual attire at a creative workshop might communicate approachability and openness to innovative ideas.

Choosing appropriate attire involves more than selecting professionally acceptable clothes—it is about considering the context of your presentation and the expectations of your audience. If you speak at a formal industry conference, traditional business attire is likely the safest choice. However, a more relaxed look might be more effective for a startup pitch to potential investors who are known for their informal culture. It is important to research the event and understand the most appropriate dress code. You can do this by asking about the demographics and typical audience that will attend. Be conscious that sometimes an audience can be more corporate and business-oriented, in which case smart business attire would be suitable. However, if your presentation or speech is lighthearted or will be more effective when the audience connects to you on a personal level, then smart casual dress code might be more appropriate. This alignment in dress code between you, your audience, and the message you want to deliver will affect your relatability and convey subconscious messages about you and your brand.

The psychology of color in your attire also plays a pivotal role in how your message is received. Colors elicit emotions, which will go a long way to establishing a relationship of trust between you and your audience, and if you have a brand, then it will be even more important. This is because there is a strong correlation between colors and brand association. You may have noticed this yourself when you think of an airline, there are distinct colors that they are associated with, from their logo to the color of the uniforms of the flight attendants, to the color of the seats inside the plane. These colors are chosen intentionally as the airline wants you to have a specific type of experience when you fly with them; some want you to have a business-like experience, others want a comforting experience, while others want to convey calm and serenity. In the same way, choosing the right colors for your presentation can subconsciously support your presentation and represent your brand. For example, incorporating red elements into your attire or presentation might be beneficial to inspire energy and action. On the other hand, if your speech intends to reassure or encourage, softer tones like blue or green might be more appropriate. It is about finding a balance that supports your message and suits your style.

It is important to choose your accessories wisely, as they can enhance your overall appearance. Accessories are essential for dressing for success and can add a touch of personality to your outfit. However, it is important that they complement your outfit without being distracting. For men, a classic watch or a subtle pair of cufflinks can add a polished touch without overwhelming the attire. For women, simple jewelry like earrings or a necklace can elegantly accentuate an outfit. Avoid overly flashy or noisy accessories that might divert attention away from your speech. Choose each piece with the aim of enhancing your overall appearance, adding to the professionalism and cohesiveness of your look.

Incorporate these elements into your public speaking engagements to make a positive first impression and build a persona that carries your message with authority and credibility. Your attire is an integral part of your presentation, a non-verbal communicator that can influence the perception and reception of your message. As you prepare for your next speaking engagement, consider what you will say, but consider how you will appear. Remember, effective communication is a blend of substance and style, and how you dress plays a crucial role in your overall impact.

MASTER THE PAUSE: TIMING FOR EFFECT

Have you sat in a speech or presentation where it feels like the presenter is speaking at 100 miles per hour, and it seems they will never stop? How did it make you feel? Overwhelmed? Not beneficial? Did your brain hurt? For an audience, all of these feelings stem from poorly placed pauses. The strategic use of pauses can be as impactful as the words themselves. They serve multiple purposes: they emphasize important points, allow the audience to absorb complex information, and create a rhythm in your delivery that enhances listener engagement. Understanding how to effectively employ pauses in your speeches is crucial for delivering your message with the intended weight and clarity. Pauses are often overlooked as a powerful tool in a speaker's arsenal. They can transform a run-on sentence into two impactful statements, turning mere information into a compelling message that resonates. When you pause, you give your audience time to ponder the importance of your last statement, thereby increasing its significance. Moreover, strategic pauses help underline your presentation's structure, marking transitions between sections and signaling shifts in topic or tone. This will help maintain audience engagement and keep your message organized and clear.

The use of pauses requires you to become comfortable with silence, and to know how to use it effectively. Begin by reading through your speech and identifying key points where a pause could enhance understanding or emphasize a particular message. Practice these moments, being mindful of how the pause feels and its effect on the delivery. Stand in front of a mirror or record your speech to observe the impact of your pauses visually and audibly. As you become more accustomed to incorporating strategic pauses, they will feel like a natural part of your speaking rhythm rather than interruptions. You can gain further insights into how to incorporate pauses and the impact this has by listening to several speeches and paying attention to when pauses are being utilized effectively (and ineffectively). One notable example is Barack Obama, who masterfully employs pauses to great effect, creating suspense or giving weight to his words. Steve Jobs was another master at this and created the right balance of suspense, excitement, and connection. Nelson Mandela would often carefully respond in interviews to keep the audience engaged and give himself the brain space to craft his response to questions with great effect. Analyzing such speeches can help you understand the timing and impact of pauses and how they can be integrated into different types of presentations to enhance your message.

Many speakers fear silence, despite the benefits, worrying that pauses may be perceived as hesitation or a lack of preparation. This fear can lead to rushed speeches where essential details are lost, and the overall message becomes less coherent. It is important to recognize the value of pauses for effective communication when trying to overcome this fear. Embracing the power of the pause allows you to transform your public speaking style.

USE HUMOR EFFECTIVELY WITHOUT BEING A COMEDIAN

Incorporating humor into your presentations can significantly enhance audience engagement and receptivity, transforming what might be a mundane topic into an enjoyable and memorable experience. However, using humor in a professional setting requires a nuanced approach to ensure it feels natural and appropriate, adding real value to your message. The key is to integrate humor in a way that complements and highlights your points, rather than overshadowing the core message of your talk.

The best place to start is to consider the context and composition of your audience when you begin. In previous chapters, I have highlighted the importance of understanding your audience prior to the speaking event to help you construct your speech. The same is true for knowing the type of humor to use for your audience. For example, if the audience is from a casual startup background, there will be a light-hearted and sometimes direct form of humor that may be suitable. If you are speaking to a more corporate formal audience, the type of humor may require a bit of whit and be indirect.

Industry-specific jokes or light-hearted anecdotes about everyday professional experiences can resonate well, making the humor feel tailored and thoughtful. However, it is crucial to be mindful of cultural differences, as they can affect how certain jokes are perceived. What may be funny in one culture could be offensive in another. For example, jokes that are fast-paced and driven by stereotypes suit an American audience well, whilst jokes with multiple levels of meaning may suit an Asian audience better; Europeans may resonate with regional satire.

The timing and delivery of humor are as important as the content. A well-timed joke after a complex slide or a humorous remark following a heavy discussion can serve as a mental break, refreshing the audience and enhancing their engagement with the material. It is about finding those moments in your presentation where a touch of humor can serve as a bridge, break down barriers and build an emotional connection with your audience. This can make you more likable and your message more persuasive. When you share a laugh with your audience, you create a moment of shared joy and camaraderie that transcends your speech and serves as a foundation for an ongoing relationship. It is essential, however, to ensure that the humor is inclusive and respectful to all audience members. The goal is to add value and enjoyment to your presentation, not to alienate or offend anyone.

While humor is effective, you should be cautious of potential pitfalls that can have the opposite effect of what was intended, creating a sense of distance. Avoid controversial topics such as politics, religion, or personal beliefs, which may lead to offensive humor, but can also detract from the main message of your presentation. Relying too heavily on humor can also be risky, as it might dilute the seriousness of your message or lead to misunderstandings if not everyone appreciates or understands the joke. Therefore, balance is crucial; use humor sparingly and strategically, ensuring it aligns with and enhances your presentation's objectives.

Plan to use humor, but try practicing in front of colleagues or friends who can provide feedback on its appropriateness and effectiveness. Practice can also help refine your timing and delivery, ensuring the humor feels natural and well-integrated into your presentation. This will amplify your message and make you more memorable and personable.

COMMAND THE STAGE WITH YOUR MOVEMENT

When you step onto the stage, you're not just a speaker; you become a performer whose stage presence can captivate or deflate the energy of a room. Establishing a commanding presence is essential—it ensures that the audience is with you from the moment you start speaking, hanging onto your every word. Your ability to manage the stage effectively is as crucial as the content of your speech because it significantly influences how that content is received. Think of the stage as an extension of your communication toolkit; moving with intention across that space can help underscore your message, making it more dynamic and memorable. Effective stage management starts with understanding how movement can enhance your message. Just as a conductor uses a baton to emphasize the music's rhythm, your movement across the stage can highlight significant parts of your presentation. For example, walking toward the audience can draw them in, making a particular point feel more intimate and urgent. Conversely, stepping back might allow the audience to reflect on what you've just said, adding weight and significance. Strategic movement requires practice and awareness of its impact—consider each step purposefully so it aligns with and amplifies the narrative flow of your message.

Navigating the space effectively, whether it is a large stage for a keynote or a smaller area for a workshop, involves an acute awareness of your environment and how your movements within that space affect audience perception. In larger venues, it is useful to use the entire stage to connect with different parts of the audience, making your presence felt throughout the room. In more intimate settings, smaller, more subtle movements can be effective. You might lean slightly forward when making an important point, using physical closeness to create a sense of immediacy and connection. Always be conscious of your positioning and movement, ensuring that they serve your message rather than distract from it.

Stage management is an art and a crucial component of effective public speaking. It requires a blend of awareness, planning, and spontaneity to elevate your presentation from a monologue to a dynamic interaction. By viewing the stage as a canvas on which your message is painted, you can use your presence and movement to draw your audience into your narrative, making it a shared and impactful experience. As you refine your stage management skills, remember that each presentation is an opportunity to experiment with and hone these techniques, ensuring that with every speech, you grow as a speaker and performer who leaves a lasting impression.

In the early stages of your public speaking career, observe the movements of seasoned speakers and performers to gain valuable insights into understanding the effect of various movements and how to incorporate them into your speech. Carefully observe how the speakers use stage space to inspire you with techniques that suit your style and context. Many skilled speakers map out their movements during their rehearsal, planning not just what they will say but also how they will physically navigate the stage during different parts of their speech. This preparation can help ensure your movements are fluid and confident rather than random or reactive. Studying performances where speakers have effectively commanded the stage can also highlight the dos and don'ts of stage movement, from maintaining open body language to avoiding turning your back to the audience.

Moving into the next chapter, we will shift our focus to using technology to enhance your presentation and take it to the next level. From integrating multimedia to leveraging social media for extended engagement, you will learn how to use digital tools to supplement your presentations and amplify and expand your reach. With technological advancements, public speaking as an art is constantly evolving, and mastering digital techniques will ensure that your skills remain cutting-edge and that your messages resonate not just in the room but around the world.

6

LEVERAGE TECHNOLOGY IN YOUR PRESENTATIONS

In the digital age, the art of public speaking transcends the mere act of speaking before an audience. Today, technology offers powerful tools that amplify your message, engage your audience more deeply, and provide dynamic ways to present complex information with clarity and impact. It is essential to understand that you can use technology before, during, and after your presentations to engage different types of audiences and for various reasons. For example, you can use a survey before your speech to understand your audience demographics or their pain points. During a presentation, you can use polling software to keep your audience engaged. After a speech, you can send a short video to thank your audience for their participation, and incorporate a call to action. These techniques can turn even a basic presentation into an immersive experience, simply because you are engaging the audience at each stage. In this chapter, I will guide you through selecting, using, and optimizing audio-visual aids to elevate your public speaking engagements. I will share why and how you can use audio-visual aids, and hone in on the most commonly used aid: a

PowerPoint presentation. Then, I will discuss some tools that will assist you to increase engagement with your audience before, during, and after your presentation. Finally, I explain how I have used virtual reality to practice speeches to reduce pre-speech anxiety, and how it can be a mechanism for self-analysis.

AUDIO-VISUAL AIDS: HOW TO USE THEM

Put simply, audio-visual aids are instructional devices that can communicate your message more effectively without having to sound it out for your audience. There are numerous aids you can employ, ranging from PowerPoint presentations and short videos to charts and diagrams. You can also incorporate sound effects or music into your presentation to build suspense or emphasize a point. However, there are three important principles to keep in mind when you incorporate an aid:

i. It should **enhance** your message.
ii. It should be **context-appropriate**.
iii. It should **maintain the flow** of your presentation.

Enhance Your Message

Audio-visual aids, when used carefully, can transform the delivery of your message and bolster audience engagement. Imagine delivering a talk on the global impact of renewable energy; a well-placed video showing the transformation of a community post-adoption of solar panels can turn abstract statistics into tangible, impactful realities. Visual aids like graphs and charts clarify and summarize complex data, enabling your audience to grasp detailed information quickly and effortlessly. The next time you have to deliver a speech, remember: a picture says a thousand words, meaning you can say more with less by incorporating diagrams, videos, charts, and more. However, if you have to explain the diagram, it might not actually enhance your message. It can be likened to someone trying to explain a joke they have just told because no one understood it. The focus shifts from the joke to the explanation and will inevitably ruin the flow of the joke. You can also use audio cues to build emotions into your presentation, whether through stirring background music during a poignant moment or audio clips from industry experts. When synchronized with your spoken words, these elements create a multi-sensory experience that facilitates greater understanding and retention of information. The goal is to make the essential parts of your message stand out and be memorable.

Make it Context Appropriate

Selecting the right audio-visual tools is key to reinforcing your message. The choice of aid should align with the specific objectives of your presentation and the needs of your audience. For instance, if you aim to explain a complex process, a step-by-step animated diagram may be more effective than a static image. Consider the venue as well; larger screens benefit big conference halls, whereas smaller, more intimate settings might benefit from tablets or interactive displays that allow for personal interaction. Always tailor your tools to the content, context, and audience demographics to ensure they add value to your presentation.

Maintain the Flow

The integration of audio-visual aids should feel seamless

and natural, enhancing the narrative flow rather than interrupting it. Plan the points in your speech where you will introduce each visual or audio element. This planning should be strategic. Use visual aids to underscore important points or represent what words alone cannot convey effectively. Practice the transitions between speaking and introducing audio-visual elements to maintain a smooth, engaging delivery. Remember, these tools are there to support your message, not to overshadow your presence as the speaker. They should complement your narrative, adding depth and dimension to your delivery rather than acting as standalone features.

By mastering the use of audio-visual aids, you not only enhance the effectiveness of your presentations but also underscore your adaptability and skill as a modern speaker. When used thoughtfully, these tools can transform simple information delivery into an engaging, memorable experience. As you continue integrating technology into your presentations, think of each tool as a component of your storytelling. Each element is a brushstroke in the larger picture you are painting with your words. In doing so, you leverage the full spectrum of possibilities technology offers, ensuring your message is heard, visually and emotionally impactful, resonating a lasting impression on your audience even after the presentation is over.

THE ESSENTIALS OF EFFECTIVE PRESENTATION SLIDES

Since Microsoft developed PowerPoint, they have become a staple in presenting and conveying ideas, strategies, and key points across almost all sectors. In more recent years, there has been a wide range of new software that have been developed, such as Canva, Prezi, Keynote, Visme and more — all with their own nuances and suitable for different purposes and skill levels. However, the effectiveness of these presentations largely depends on their design and execution. Adhering to basic design principles ensures your slides capture and hold the attention of your audience. These principles are about aesthetics, as well as crafting slides that enhance the viewer's ability to absorb and retain information efficiently.

When designing slides, clarity, and impact are the cornerstones. Design each slide to communicate one idea or concept. Overloading slides with multiple ideas can confuse and overwhelm your audience, distracting them from your message. Use a clean layout with plenty of white or neutral colored space, which helps to reduce visual clutter and focuses the attention of the audience on the content that matters. Consistent use of fonts, colors, and styles throughout the presentation are essential to maintain a professional look while reinforcing the coherence of your message. For instance, select a sans-serif font for readability and use no more than three different font sizes: one for headers, one for subheaders, and one for body text.

Balancing text and visuals is another critical aspect of an effective design. While text provides the necessary details, visuals can illustrate and enhance these points, making them more memorable. However, striking the right balance is crucial. Slides should not be text heavy as large blocks of text can be daunting and likely disengage your audience. Instead, aim to use visuals such as graphs, charts, images, or icons to support or explain your main ideas. Bullet points are outdated for displaying text on slides, so it is best to use them sparingly or avoid them altogether. This approach breaks down the information into digestible chunks and caters to visual learners, making your presentation more inclusive.

Animations and transitions are tools that, when used in

small quantities, can significantly but indirectly and subtly emphasize the transition of your message. The key is to use animation to spotlight important points or to show changes over time, such as the progression of sales data in a line graph. Avoid overly complex or whimsical animations that take focus away from the content. Subtle effects like 'Fade' or 'Wipe' can effectively transition between slides or reveal important points without the excessive flair that might make your presentation seem less professional. Navigating the slides smoothly is equally important as the content you display because disruptive or erratic navigation will throw off your rhythm and result in your audience losing focus. It would be best if you gave ample time in your preparation for the speech to familiarize yourself with the presentation's flow beforehand to ensure a seamless delivery. Learn to use the presenter view on your chosen software, as it allows you to see your notes on one screen while the audience sees only the slide on the other. This feature can be incredibly beneficial in maintaining your train of thought without displaying your notes to the audience. Additionally, be prepared for unexpected technical issues by having a backup plan. This might include having a PDF version of your presentation on a USB drive or ensuring an online version can be accessed quickly from any device.

By meticulously designing your slides to balance aesthetics with functionality and thoroughly preparing for delivery, you can ensure that your presentations capture and hold your audience's attention throughout your session. Remember, a well-crafted slide presentation can be a powerful tool for communicating your message and making your ideas more transparent and persuasive to your audience.

1. **Compatibility**

It is important that the polling software be compatible with your presentation and the hardware available at your venue. You'll want a platform that integrates seamlessly with common presentation software and is responsive across multiple device types, ensuring that all audience members can participate regardless of their device.

2. **User interface**

Your audience's experience is essential to obtaining the intended results of a two-way conversation. Opt for intuitive, easy-to-use software with clear instructions and a simple response mechanism. Your audience's time is valuable, and poll participation should be quick and hassle-free.

3. **Privacy**

Keep anonymity and privacy at the forefront, especially in sensitive environments by ensuring the software provides options for anonymous responses if needed. You will often find that a portion of the audience will be vocal, but a larger proportion will be more reluctant to share their answers openly, for any number of reasons.

The use of polls in your presentation should be strategic and purposeful. Start your session with a quick poll to capture attention and set the tone for participation. Use polls to transition between segments, engage the audience, and summarize opinions. Clearly explain the purpose of each poll and how results will influence the session. Analyze and respond to poll results in real-time for immediate feedback. Use results to tailor future presentations for better effectiveness.

PRACTICE YOUR SPEECH WITH VIRTUAL REALITY

Integrating virtual reality (VR) as a rehearsal tool in public speaking can transform how speakers prepare and refine their delivery before stepping onto a real stage. The immersive nature of VR provides a unique platform that simulates various speaking environments, allowing you to practice in a controlled yet realistic setting. This technology offers several distinct advantages for public speakers, regardless of their experience level.

One of the most significant benefits of using VR for speech rehearsal is the ability to simulate diverse audiences and venues. Imagine standing in a virtual conference room or a packed auditorium with a responsive audience, all from the comfort of your home or office. VR platforms can mimic different audience sizes, reactions, and even interjections, providing a dynamic environment to practice your delivery and timing. This realistic simulation enhances your adaptability and boosts your confidence, as you can rehearse in contexts that closely resemble the real-life scenarios you will face. Furthermore, VR allows you to experience and manage stage presence in various settings, helping you develop flexibility in your speaking style and adapt to different audience dynamics.

Accessing suitable VR tools for speech practice involves considering several factors, including the software's compatibility with your hardware, the realism of the simulation, and the specific features it offers for public speaking training. Start by researching VR platforms that are designed specifically for public speaking. Platforms like VirtualSpeech or Ovation are tailored to help speakers hone their skills by providing realistic environments and audience interactions.

These tools often come with features such as audience reaction metrics, speech analysis, and even feedback on your pacing and use of filler words.

To choose the right VR platform, assess your specific needs—such as the type of presentations you usually give, the typical size of your audiences, and the areas where you feel you need the most practice. Additionally, ensure that your hardware can support these applications. Most VR systems require a compatible headset and sometimes additional computing power to run smoothly.

The potential for receiving feedback in VR environments is one of the most transformative aspects of refining your presentation skills. Advanced VR platforms incorporate artificial intelligence to provide real-time feedback on various elements of your speech, including voice clarity, volume, modulation, and body language. This immediate feedback enables you to make adjustments and practice those improvements, reinforcing learning and skill development in a way traditional rehearsal methods cannot match. Moreover, some VR systems can record your sessions, allowing for further review and analysis. You can watch your performance and critically assess your delivery, gestures, and audience engagement strategies. This kind of detailed feedback is invaluable as it allows you to see yourself from the audience's perspective, giving you a clearer understanding of areas for improvement.

VIDEO RECORDING YOUR SPEECH FOR SELF-ANALYSIS

In the pursuit of refining your public speaking skills, video recording stands out as an invaluable tool, and offers a mirror to view your performance through the eyes of your audience.

This technique allows for an objective analysis of your delivery and content, providing insights often missed in the immediacy of live presentation feedback. The primary benefit of this practice is the ability to see yourself as others see you. It is one thing to feel how you performed, but another to visually confirm it. You can observe many nuances in your performance by watching your recorded speeches, from pacing and gestures to facial expressions and audience interaction that you would not have otherwise noticed. This self-observation encourages a deeper understanding of your public speaking style, including strengths you can build upon and weaknesses that require attention, as well as a unique opportunity to observe and critique your performance, an exercise that is fundamental in developing your public speaking acumen. For example, you might be prone to repetitive body movements or filler words like "um" and "ah" that you weren't aware of during the live presentation. It is essential to identify these habits as a first step before correcting them, and thereafter allow for a more polished and professional delivery.

When reviewing your recordings, focus on your delivery as well as the content of your speech. Delivery encompasses your body language, vocal tone, and overall energy, which are critical to keeping your audience engaged. Look for congruence between your verbal and non-verbal cues and determine if your gestures reinforce or detract from what you're saying. As mentioned in Chapter Five, your vocal delivery will play a significant role in how your message is received, so you will also need to check for modulation, volume, and clarity. Content analysis, on the other hand, should focus on the structure of your speech, the clarity of your main points, and the effectiveness of your core message. Assess whether you articulated the key points of your presentation clearly and if the supporting information was persuasive and relevant. This dual focus helps craft how you say things and what you say, ensuring both are optimized for maximum impact. However, it is important not to try to observe all these things simultaneously otherwise you will be overwhelmed. Break this analysis into different parts and consider watching the recording three or four times to maximize your analysis.

While self-assessment is crucial, external perspectives provide additional insights you might have overlooked, so seeking external feedback on your video recordings can further enhance the value of this exercise. Try to share your recordings with trusted colleagues or mentors who understand your speaking goals and ask for their honest feedback by requesting specific information on areas of your performance, such as body language, use of space, and audience engagement. This can provide a new lens to view your performance, offering constructive criticism that fosters growth and improvement.

Once you have collated the information from your self-analysis and external feedback, you can create a targeted improvement plan based on insights gained from video analysis. It is essential to turn feedback into actionable results. Start by listing specific areas where improvement is needed, such as reducing filler words, improving eye contact, or enhancing the storytelling aspect of your speeches. Then, set realistic goals for each area by outlining steps to achieve these goals. You can create a plan where you target specific areas of improvement, like practising incorporating certain gestures, working on voice modulation exercises, or rewriting parts of your speech to enhance clarity. You can benefit further if you revisit your improvement plan to gauge progress and adjust as needed. This structured approach will help to systematically improve your public speaking skills and provide a measurable way to track your growth over time. Incorporating video recording into your preparation and review process will transform each speaking engagement into a learning opportunity and allow you to refine your skills continuously, contributing to your long-term development as a confident, powerful speaker. As you move forward, let each recording be a stepping stone to greater achievements in your public speaking journey, equipped with the tools and insights needed to captivate and engage your audience with each word you deliver.

HANDLE TECHNICAL DIFFICULTIES GRACEFULLY

One of the challenges we will often face is when our technology just won't cooperate. The younger generation who grew up with technology as a natural part of life, might not find this to be much of an issue, but those who grew up before the technology boom and had to learn how to use it might feel entirely different. However, the mere thought of having to prepare a PowerPoint, connect a laptop to the projector, navigate the slides, and then deliver the presentation can make anyone anxious. It is even more daunting when one considers the possibility that technology can fail. While technical issues are inevitable, it is your ability to handle these situations gracefully and maintain control under pressure that will reflect your professionalism and expertise. Preparing for potential glitches involves more than just understanding your presentation tools; it requires a comprehensive strategy that includes backup systems, rehearsals, and a solid plan to keep your audience engaged despite disruptions. More importantly, it will ease your anxieties and allow you to focus on delivering the best presentation possible.

The first element in this preparation process is to build

redundancy into every part of your technical setup. This means having backups for your backups. If you're using a laptop for a presentation, ensure there's another one ready to go with all necessary files loaded or upload your slides to cloud-based software, such as Dropbox or Google Drive, to enable easy access from any device. This way, even if all local copies fail, you can still retrieve your work remotely. While the hosting venue often provides technical hardware such as microphones, projectors, and presentation clickers, be sure to confirm they have a backup solution if any of their equipment fails. Moreover, familiarize yourself with the setup and functionalities of the venue's audio-visual system before the event and know whom to contact immediately for specific technical issues to expedite resolutions and minimize downtime.

The second element is to maintain your composure when technical issues arise, as it sets the tone for how the audience reacts. If you appear flustered or annoyed, it can amplify the negative impact of the disruption. Instead, stay calm and collected, even if you feel flustered internally. It takes practice to remain calm, but you can prepare for this in your visualization phase, where you should try to imagine how you will handle technical difficulties. It may be an opportunity to engage with your audience—perhaps through an impromptu Q&A about a previous point in your presentation or by sharing an interesting anecdote related to your topic. This keeps the audience engaged and gives you a buffer to resolve the issue without rushing. Your ability to remain composed under stress can enhance the audience's perception of you as a confident and capable leader.

The third element is to educate yourself with a set of quick fixes for common problems. For instance, if there's a sudden incompatibility between your presentation device and the projector, know a few basic troubleshooting steps, like adjusting the display settings or checking the HDMI connection. For audio problems, ensure you know how to adjust the microphone settings or the speaker configuration quickly. It is also helpful to understand the software you're using for presentations, which you can learn from a few YouTube videos. Familiarity with these common issues enables you to minimize the impact of the technical glitches and gives you confidence that you will manage, but also build your reputation as a capable and well-rounded individual, capable of gracefully problem-solving in unexpected circumstances.

7
REAL-WORLD APPLICATION AND COMMON SCENARIOS

Imagine standing in a bustling conference hall, the session breaks, and suddenly, you are asked to fill in for a missing speaker. The topic is familiar, but the notice is minimal. This is your moment to shine, not with prepared words but with the ability to think on your feet. Or you were booked for the small seminar room you normally speak in, but the registered attendance for your event was unexpectedly high, meaning the location of your speech was moved to the large theatre seating 300 people. Or you were informed there would be a short Q&A session with a panel at the end of your speech. These scenarios are not just hypothetical; they are a real part of public speaking engagements. In this chapter, I will share some insights on how I became comfortable with impromptu speeches, set up some principles to be able to adapt to any speaking environment, navigated difficult Q&A sessions, and also refined my elevator pitch for maximum impact.

THE ART OF THE IMPROMPTU SPEECH

Delivering an unexpected speech without prior preparation or notes is a skill in itself. Unlike prepared speeches, which allow time for meticulous planning and rehearsal, impromptu speeches require the speaker to think on their feet and articulate their thoughts clearly and coherently on the spot. This form of speaking is common in professional and social settings, manifesting in sudden requests to share opinions in meetings, toasts at celebrations, or responses during interviews, to give a few examples. However, it is important to know that while it is unexpected, you can and should prepare for these, because you must equip yourself with the skills to communicate effectively and confidently in any situation. Being adept at speaking spontaneously enhances your ability to respond thoughtfully and persuasively, leaving a positive impression on your audience. Moreover, it demonstrates your quick thinking and adaptability, valuable traits in today's fast-paced, dynamic environments. Mastering the art of improvisation can significantly elevate your professional and personal interactions, ensuring you are always ready to convey your message with clarity and impact. In this segment, I will share some of the basic but essential components of this art that you can practice.

Structure Thoughts Quickly

When called upon to speak without prior notice, the first challenge you face is organizing your thoughts swiftly and effectively. Begin by quickly outlining a basic structure in your mind:

i. Start with a clear introduction where you state the topic and your key message.
ii. Proceed with two or three main points.
iii. Conclude with a summary or a call to action.

This simple structure provides a skeleton on which to flesh out your speech. Practice the "What, Why, How" strategy in your daily communications to help this rapid structuring. What is the topic? Why is it important? How does it affect your audience? Regularly thinking along these lines outside of speaking engagements prepares you to structure impromptu speeches effectively, ensuring your content is organized and impactful.

Embracing Spontaneity

Improvisation can be your greatest ally if harnessed correctly, as it brings a fresh and genuine energy to your speech, which can resonate well with the audience. To embrace it, you must shift your mindset to view impromptu speaking opportunities as a chance to engage and connect rather than a trial to endure. You can try exercises such as spontaneously speaking on random topics or engaging in rapid-fire question-and-answer sessions to develop a degree of comfort with spontaneity. These exercises train your mind to formulate quick responses and adapt your message on the fly, which are invaluable skills in impromptu speaking scenarios.

Build a Mental Repository

A well-prepared speaker is always ready, even at a

moment's notice, so you need to create and continuously expand a bank of anecdotes, statistics, quotes, and industry facts. This repository becomes your go-to resource to enrich your speech or back your points with credible information. To build this repository, make it a habit to read widely and deeply across various subjects, particularly those relevant to your field. Take notes on exciting or significant information that you can seamlessly integrate into your conversations. Over time, retrieving this information during your speeches will become second nature, allowing you to speak with authority and depth, even without preparation.

Confidence in the Unexpected

Confidence is crucial, especially when the unexpected call to speak arises. It stems from a combination of preparedness and practice. Regularly put yourself in situations where you need to speak without preparation, perhaps in meetings or social gatherings. Additionally, focus on developing a positive speaking mindset, visualizing successful speech outcomes regularly, and reflecting on positive feedback from past speaking engagements to reinforce your self-belief.

By approaching impromptu speaking with an understanding of the above components, you naturally build confidence, which allows you to handle unexpected situations with poise and assurance. Your ability to communicate effectively at a moment's notice can significantly enhance your credibility and influence and open doors for unexpected opportunities. As you refine the skills discussed, remember that each impromptu speaking opportunity is a chance to demonstrate your expertise and confidence.

ADAPTING YOUR SPEECH FOR DIFFERENT VENUES AND FORMATS

When you step into different speaking environments, from the echoing halls of a conference center to the intimate setting of a boardroom, or a digital platform with virtual audiences, the effectiveness of your delivery can hinge significantly on how well you adapt your speech to these varying contexts. Understanding the nuances of each venue and the expectations of different formats is crucial in ensuring your message lands and resonates deeply with your audience. Each venue has challenges and opportunities - mastering these can elevate public speaking from good to unforgettable. I will share with you some of the key areas to be aware of and create a plan for how you will navigate the challenges, with consideration of the necessary mindset, content preparation, delivery, and audience participation.

Venue Variability

The physical or virtual setup of a venue is pivotal in how your speech is received. In a large conference hall, your voice needs to project confidence and strength, reaching the back of the room without losing the intimacy that connects you with your audience. Here, aspects like microphone technique and strategic pauses to allow your words to resonate become crucial. On the other hand, in a smaller, more intimate venue, such as a corporate boardroom, the tone can shift to a conversational style, fostering a dialogue rather than a monologue. This setup often allows for immediate feedback and interaction, which can be leveraged to create a dynamic exchange of ideas. Virtual formats present a different challenge, as you need to engage an audience you cannot see, demanding a higher energy level, as well as the use of visual aids and interactive tools to maintain engagement across the digital divide. Adapting to each venue involves technical adjustments and a recalibration of your delivery style to suit the environment and audience dynamics.

Format Adaptation

The format of your presentation can vary widely, from educational workshops to persuasive sales pitches or inspirational TEDx talks. Each format demands a different approach to how your content is structured and delivered. Clarity and progression are essential in educational settings, ensuring the audience can follow along and absorb information effectively. For persuasive presentations, such as sales pitches, the emphasis might shift toward building a compelling narrative that leads to a robust call to action. Inspirational talks, like those on a TEDx stage, often rely heavily on personal stories and emotional engagement, requiring a deep connection with the audience that transcends the mere transfer of information. Adapting your speech to fit these formats involves tailoring your content and fine-tuning your delivery to meet the specific objectives of the format as well as the expectations of the audience.

Engagement Techniques

Engaging your audience effectively requires versatility and a keen sense of observation. Techniques that work well in one venue might be less effective in another. In larger venues, direct interaction with the audience might include polling the audience or directing questions to different sections of the room to maintain engagement across the space. In contrast, smaller venues allow for more direct and personal engagement techniques, such as round-table discussions or interactive Q&A sessions, which can foster a closer connection and more immediate engagement. Virtual environments call for creativity—incorporating live chats, interactive polls, or breakout rooms can help mimic the interactive experience of a physical venue. The key to successful engagement across different venues lies in your ability to flexibly adjust your techniques to align with your physical proximity with the audience.

PRACTICAL STRATEGIES FOR ADAPTING YOUR SPEECH

Mindset Preparation

1. **Visualization**

Practice visualizing yourself in different speaking environments. Imagine the room layout, the reactions of the audience, and your movements and gestures. This mental rehearsal helps reduce anxiety and builds confidence for any venue. It is well known that Steve Jobs famously prepared for his iconic product launches by rehearsing in an empty theater, visualizing every detail, from the lighting to the audience's reactions. This meticulous preparation helped him deliver memorable presentations.

2. **Flexibility**

Cultivate a mindset of flexibility and one that can

embrace change. Practice delivering parts of your speech in different settings and scenarios. For example, try presenting a segment of your speech outdoors, in a crowded room, or a quiet office. This practice helps you adapt seamlessly to various environments. You can also try practicing while you walk through your house, or a public garden, where the scenery is constantly changing. This will have a subconscious effect, enabling you to become comfortable with change. Oprah Winfrey's ability to connect with diverse audiences, whether in a large studio or an intimate interview setting, stems from her practice of adapting her delivery to the environment, making every audience feel seen and heard.

Content Preparation

1. Tailored Content

Adapt your content to fit the venue. For large venues, focus on broad, impactful statements and visuals that can be seen from a distance. For intimate settings, include more detailed anecdotes and data points that invite closer scrutiny and interaction. Barack Obama is an excellent example of someone who's speeches varied greatly depending on the venue. In large stadiums, he used powerful, overarching themes and striking visuals. In smaller town hall meetings and engaged in direct dialogue with the audience, sharing personal stories.

2. Multimedia Use

Prepare multimedia elements that can be easily adjusted based on the venue. For instance, slides that work well on a large screen can be simplified for smaller screens or even adapted for virtual backgrounds in online presentations. If you want to see this in practice, look up some TED Talks, as they often incorporate multimedia elements to enhance their message. Speakers like Sir Ken Robinson have used simple yet effective visuals that resonate in both live and online formats, amplifying their impact.

Delivery Techniques

1. Voice Modulation

Practice varying your voice volume and pitch to suit different venues. In a large hall, work on projecting your voice clearly without shouting. In smaller rooms, focus on softer tones and more conversational delivery. Martin Luther King Jr.'s 'I Have a Dream' speech exemplifies a powerful voice modulation. He used varying pitch and volume to captivate a large audience on the National Mall, ensuring his message reached everyone.

2. Body Language

Adapt your body language to fit the space. In large venues, use broader gestures and move around the stage to engage the entire audience. Use more subtle gestures and maintain eye contact in smaller venues to create a closer connection. Tony Robbins, a renowned motivational speaker, is an excellent example of how to adapt one's body language and movement to suit your audience. He used expansive gestures and high energy in large seminars to engage thousands, while in smaller workshops, his approach was more personal and interactive.

Audience Participation

1. **Interactive Elements**

Incorporate interactive elements that suit the venue. Consider using audience response systems or mobile apps for large audiences for real-time polling. In smaller settings, encourage direct questions and discussions to foster engagement. Simon Sinek's workshops often include interactive exercises, regardless of the venue size. In large conferences, he uses technology to gather audience input. In smaller settings, he facilitates group activities and discussions to deepen engagement.

2. **Adaptable Engagement**

Prepare different engagement techniques for various formats. Use features like breakout rooms, live chats, and polls for virtual presentations. For physical venues, adapt to the space by moving closer to the audience or adjusting your position to enhance interaction. During the COVID-19 pandemic, many speakers like Brené Brown successfully transitioned to virtual formats, using interactive tools and live feedback to maintain the connection with their audience, proving that engagement can transcend physical barriers.

HANDLE DIFFICULT QUESTIONS AND INTERRUPTIONS WITH EASE

One of the inevitable parts of public speaking is being asked difficult questions or even being interrupted and heckled by the crowd, and it would even fluster seasoned public speakers if not anticipated. In this segment, I want to share how navigating challenging questions or unexpected interruptions during a speech can supercharge your credibility and authority as a speaker, even if the prospect of doing so is daunting. Preparation is essential, and having a robust strategy not only helps you to respond effectively, it also maintains the flow of your presentation. I have outlined my three-step strategy for this below.

Anticipate and Prepare

Preparation is a fundamental aspect in anticipating potential skeptics in your audience who may disrupt your flow or ask the tough questions at the end. To overcome this, begin by understanding your subject matter in depth and comb through your speech to identify areas where you may be questioned. This can be based on definitions you have used, assumptions you have incorporated into your presentation, and data that you have leaned on. Start by anticipating potential questions or scenarios based on these aspects and other potential areas. The next step is to prepare clear, concise responses and consider different angles from which your audience might approach these topics. This preparatory step ensures you're not caught off-guard and can provide thoughtful, composed responses. If you sit down to anticipate and prepare this way, the chances of getting questions that are curveballs will be slim, and when those do come up, you can always tell the questioner that you will revert back to them.

Maintain Composure

Maintaining composure during these moments is crucial and can significantly impact how your audience perceives your expertise and confidence. Hence, you must develop a calm demeanor by practising stress-reduction techniques such as deep breathing or positive affirmations before your presentations. Then, if you are faced with a tricky question or unwarranted interruption, take a moment to collect your thoughts. A short pause helps you gather your thoughts and shows the audience that you are considering their query seriously. Address the person with respect and maintain eye contact; this indicates that you value their contribution and are in control of the situation. Remember, how you respond to these challenges often speaks louder than the answers you provide.

Redirect to Key Messages

Redirecting questions or interruptions back to your key messages is an art that keeps your presentation on track. When you encounter a question that deviates significantly from the topic, acknowledge it but bridge it back to your main points. For instance, if asked about a loosely related technical detail, you might say, "That's an interesting aspect, but let's focus on how it impacts our main discussion today..." This technique lets you acknowledge the audience's interests without derailing your planned presentation. Weaving statements reinforcing your key messages helps steer the conversation back to your primary objectives.

Practical Scenario

Consider a scenario in which you present a new marketing strategy, and an audience member interrupts with a detailed question about a minor aspect of the data you presented.

Here's how to handle it:

i. Acknowledge the question: "That's a great observation on the data point..."
ii. Provide a brief and precise answer: Address the query directly but succinctly.
iii. Redirect to the broader strategy: "...and this ties back to our larger goal of increasing market penetration."

Through such interactions, you address the audience's queries and keep the presentation aligned with your objectives.

By equipping yourself with the ability to handle difficult questions and interruptions gracefully and effectively, you will maintain the flow and integrity of your presentation and enhance your stature as a knowledgeable and confident speaker. As you continue to engage in public speaking, view each difficult question or interruption as an opportunity to reinforce your key messages and connect with your audience on a deeper level. Remember that no matter how hard the question is, stay composed, acknowledge the question, and respond genuinely.

REFINE YOUR ELEVATOR PITCH

Crafting an effective elevator pitch is essential in the fast-paced environments of networking events where making a memorable first impression is crucial. The goal is simple: within a brief interaction, your pitch must capture interest and concisely convey the core value of your business or personal brand. To begin crafting your elevator pitch, start with a clear understanding of your aim.

Are you seeking a new job, looking for investors, or simply trying to expand your professional network? Once your objective is defined, distil the essence of what you do into a single, impactful sentence. This statement should encapsulate what sets you or your business apart from others. Next, expand this sentence into a short narrative that includes who you are, what you do, why it is unique, and what you are looking for or offering. For example, suppose you are a digital marketing expert specializing in startup branding. In that case, your pitch might start with, "I help new tech startups establish their brand presence online with cutting-edge digital strategies that have already doubled the online traffic for several early-stage companies."

Understanding the key components that make an elevator pitch successful is critical. It should be succinct, usually at most 30-60 seconds, compelling, and tailored to provoke further conversation. It should also include a hook that grabs attention, details that invite curiosity, and a closing that leaves room for follow-up. The hook could be an intriguing statistic or a bold claim about your results. The details might outline how your approach is innovative or different. The closing should be an invitation to continue the conversation, perhaps by exchanging business cards or arranging a follow-up meeting. Ensuring clarity and enthusiasm in your delivery is paramount; if you are not excited about what you are saying, your listener will not be either. Rehearsing helps refine your delivery to ensure clarity and confidence, which are both vital in making your pitch compelling. So it is important to practice, analyze and refine your delivery.

Adapting your elevator pitch to match the interests and needs of your audience is also crucial. This requires quick thinking and a keen sense of observation. At the start of any networking interaction, take a moment to gauge the interest and background of your conversation partner. Use questions to draw out information that can help you tailor your pitch on the spot. For instance, if you learn that the person is interested in sustainability and your business has an eco-friendly product line, you can emphasize that aspect in your pitch. This adaptability makes your pitch more relevant and shows your attentiveness and capability to customize solutions based on client needs.

Effective follow-up strategies are essential to capitalize on successful elevator pitch encounters. After your initial interaction, note what was discussed, and any details that can help personalize future communications. Send a follow-up email within 24-48 hours to express your appreciation for the conversation and suggest a next step. This could be a meeting, a phone call, or a link to further information about your business or project. Keeping momentum is vital to transforming a brief encounter into a lasting business relationship.

In real-world applications, a well-crafted elevator pitch can open doors in various scenarios beyond traditional networking events. Whether it is a chance meeting with a potential client in a coffee shop, a quick introduction during a workshop break, or an impromptu conversation during a community gathering, your elevator pitch is a powerful tool to create opportunities for professional growth and collaboration. Each interaction is a chance to refine and perfect your pitch, making it an indispensable component of your professional toolkit, ready to be deployed whenever the opportunity arises.

POSITION YOURSELF AS A THOUGHT LEADER IN PANEL DISCUSSIONS

When you engage in panel discussions, you are offered a platform to share insights and significantly boost your status as a leader in your field. Adequate preparation for these discussions is more than just understanding the topic at hand. This involves deep research into the backgrounds of your fellow panelists and the questions that might arise during the discussion. This preparatory work enables you to tailor your contributions to complement the expertise of your co-panelists, thereby enhancing the coherence and depth of the debate. Review recent articles, books, or interviews featuring your fellow panelists to grasp their views and perspectives. This understanding allows you to build on their statements constructively or, when necessary, politely counter them with well-founded arguments. Additionally, anticipate potential questions from the audience by considering current trends and hot topics within your industry and preparing your responses to align with your key messages and professional ethos.

Expressing your opinions with confidence is crucial in asserting your thought leadership during these discussions. It is important to articulate your ideas clearly and assertively, backing them up with data, anecdotes, or case studies that reinforce your points. Practice your key points in advance, focusing on delivering them confidently and clearly. However, confidence should not be confused with rigidity. The true skill lies in presenting your ideas flexibly and adapting your message in response to the flow of the discussion, thus demonstrating both your depth of knowledge and adaptability. This approach positions you as an expert and a dynamic thinker capable of engaging critically with evolving industry challenges.

Effective interaction with fellow panelists and the audience can transform a simple discussion into a compelling exchange of ideas. Foster a collegial atmosphere by actively listening to your co-panelist, responding to their points thoughtfully, and linking their insights to your own. This creates a seamless dialogue that enhances the value for the audience. Moreover, directly engage with the audience by inviting questions and responding thoughtfully. Use these interactions as opportunities to delve deeper into your subject matter expertise, demonstrating your commitment to addressing the audience's interests and concerns.

Defining and establishing yourself as a thought leader goes beyond sharing knowledge; it involves inspiring and influencing others. Thought leadership involves pioneering ideas, sparking discussions, and leading initiatives that drive your industry forward. It is about being seen as a credible resource in your field, someone who predicts trends and contributes to shaping them. Use panel discussions as a stage to showcase this leadership. Share visionary ideas, challenge conventional thinking where appropriate, and provide unique solutions to industry problems. Try to reflect on successful thought leaders who have utilized public speaking effectively to cement their status in their industries. These individuals often use panel discussions to inform and inspire action and innovation. They are remembered for what they said and the impact of their words on their audience and industry. Emulate these qualities in your discussions by being informative, inspirational, and influential.

To conclude, remember that every panel discussion is an opportunity to reinforce your position as a thought leader. Each element should be aligned to strengthen your professional reputation and influence. As you continue participating in these discussions, keep refining your skills and stay informed and responsive to the latest trends and changes within your field. This ongoing commitment to growth and engagement defines and sustains a thought leader.

The next chapter will explore advanced public speaking

strategies, delving into innovative techniques to enhance your impact and effectiveness as a speaker. This will include exploring new technologies, advanced rhetorical methods, and unique presentation styles that can set you apart in any speaking engagement.

8
CONTINUOUS IMPROVEMENT AND ADVANCED STRATEGIES

The most successful speakers view each presentation as an integral part of a continual journey of growth and refinement. Just as skilled artisans never stop refining their craft, proficient speakers must consistently seek new ways to enhance their skills. As you refine your skills and broaden your reach, incorporating feedback, mastering advanced storytelling techniques, using technology, and expanding your presence beyond the stage becomes paramount. This chapter delves into these critical areas, offering practical strategies to elevate your public speaking prowess to new heights.

INCORPORATE FEEDBACK FOR ONGOING IMPROVEMENT

Creating a Feedback Loop

To establish a structured feedback loop, you need a clear intention to improve, so you can consider every speech an opportunity to gather insights to refine your speaking abilities. Once you put this hat on, you should start by encouraging feedback in different forms; this can be as simple as distributing feedback forms, setting up digital surveys post-presentation, or inviting the audience to give verbal feedback in smaller settings. The key is to make this process a standard part of your speaking engagements, signaling to your audience that you value their input and are committed to continuous improvement. Additionally, involve your peers and mentors in this feedback loop. They can offer professional insights that audience members may not perceive, providing a balanced view encompassing listener impact and technical effectiveness.

Analyzing Feedback

Once you have gathered feedback, the next step is its analysis. Approach this phase with an open mind, ready to extract actionable insights rather than justifications. Categorize the feedback into themes—perhaps delivery, content clarity, or audience engagement. This segmentation helps identify patterns and common areas needing attention. For a more objective analysis, consider using quantitative methods like scoring systems or qualitative methods like thematic analysis for open-ended responses. This structured approach helps pinpoint specific areas where changes can yield the most significant impact, transforming raw data into a roadmap for improvement.

Actionable Improvement Plans

With a clear understanding of what needs improvement, you can develop an actionable plan that targets these areas.

Set specific, measurable goals for each key theme identified in the feedback. For instance, if increasing audience engagement is a goal, one action might be to incorporate more rhetorical questions or interactive elements into your next speech. Each goal should have clear steps and a timeline, making the improvement process structured and trackable. Regularly review and adjust these plans based on ongoing feedback to ensure they remain relevant and effectively drive your development as a speaker.

Celebrate Your Progress

Recognition of progress is as crucial as the process of improvement itself. Celebrating milestones boosts your motivation and reinforces the value of the feedback loop. Acknowledge improvements in your public speaking skills in newsletters or social media updates, sharing your journey with your audience or peers. This serves as personal motivation and encourages a culture of continuous improvement among your peers and followers. Recognizing and sharing these achievements highlights the iterative nature of mastering public speaking, where each step forward is a building block in the edifice of your speaking prowess.

Embracing feedback as an important element of your speaking engagements encourages you to unlock the potential for continual growth. This process transforms every presentation into a steppingstone towards excellence, ensuring that your journey in public speaking is marked by constant evolution and marked improvements. By integrating feedback deeply into your practice, you enhance your skills and model a commitment to excellence that can inspire and educate others in your field. Each piece of feedback, each plan for improvement, and each celebration of progress is a testament to your dedication to participating in the public speaking space as well as thriving within it by continually pushing the boundaries of what you can achieve.

ADVANCED STORYTELLING TECHNIQUES FOR SEASONED SPEAKERS

As you advance in your public speaking career, the depth and complexity of your storytelling should grow to reflect your expanding expertise and understanding of your audience. Delving into sophisticated narrative arcs and character development can transform your presentations from informative to unforgettable. Complex narrative arcs involve structures beyond the simple beginning-middle-end format and may incorporate multiple intertwined threads, flashbacks, or non-linear timelines. These can be particularly effective in keeping your audience engaged throughout your presentation, as they create suspense and a sense of journey within your story. To master these arcs, begin by sketching out the key points you want to convey, then think about how these can be interlinked or revealed in a non-sequential manner that adds intrigue or surprise. For instance, you might start with an anecdote unrelated to your main topic, gradually reveal its relevance as your presentation progresses, and finally tie all the elements together in a powerful conclusion.

Developing characters within your stories can also significantly enhance their impact. Even in business settings, character-driven stories help humanize abstract concepts and data, making them more relatable and memorable. When developing characters, focus on their motivations, challenges, and growth, which should mirror or contrast the journey you want your audience to undertake. For instance, if your goal is to inspire innovation, you might tell the story of a well-known innovator, highlighting the personal and professional hurdles they overcame. This approach deepens emotional engagement and provides a narrative framework that encourages your audience to see themselves within the story, pondering their potential for innovation and growth.

Emotional engagement is the cornerstone of compelling storytelling. It transforms your speech from a mere transfer of information to an experience that moves the audience. Techniques to enhance this engagement include using vivid language that appeals to the senses, crafting moments of tension and relief, and utilizing pacing to build and release emotional energy. Consider the emotional arc of your story as carefully as the narrative arc. Plan for moments of emotional impact - revelations, personal admissions, or dramatic illustrations of your points. The goal is to synchronize the emotional rhythms of your story with the intellectual points you are making so that your audience understands and feels your message deeply.

Incorporating multimedia elements into your stories can amplify their richness and impact. Visual aids like images, videos, or dynamic infographics can help illustrate complex points and add an emotional punch. For instance, if you are discussing the impact of climate change, a striking video showing the effects on a specific community can be more impactful than simply quoting statistics. Similarly, background music or sound effects can heighten the emotional atmosphere or underscore critical moments in your narrative. When selecting multimedia elements, ensure they are seamlessly integrated and enhance the story rather than distract from it. Each aspect should feel like a natural extension of the narrative, adding a layer of depth or emphasis that words alone might not achieve.

Analyzing the techniques used by master storytellers can

provide valuable insights into the craft of advanced storytelling. Take the time to study speeches by renowned speakers within your field or beyond. Pay attention to how they structure their stories, the types of characters they introduce, their pacing, their use of language, and how they integrate multimedia elements. Dissecting these elements can offer you a toolkit of techniques to adapt and apply in your presentations. Remember, the goal is not to mimic these masters but to learn from their techniques and adapt them in ways that align with your unique style and the needs of your audience.

By embracing these advanced storytelling techniques, you elevate your public speaking to an art form that informs, inspires, and resonates. Whether through complex narrative arcs, character development, emotional engagement, or the strategic use of multimedia, each element you master adds a new dimension to your presentations, making them heard, felt, and remembered. As you refine your storytelling skills, remember that each presentation is an opportunity to speak and to move and transform your audience.

LEVERAGE TECHNOLOGY: APPS AND TOOLS FOR SPEAKERS

In an era where technology permeates every aspect of our lives, public speaking has also seen a revolutionary shift with the advent of various high-tech tools and applications designed to refine and enhance communication. These technological aids are not just accessories; they are essential tools that can transform the traditional paradigm of public speaking into a dynamic interaction between speaker and audience. Let us explore how these technologies can be integrated into your public speaking practice, delivery, and feedback mechanisms to elevate your presentations to new heights.

Firstly, consider the vast array of apps and tools available specifically crafted to assist speakers in preparation and delivery. Apps like Speechmaker allow you to script, practice, and time your speeches, ensuring you deliver them with precision. Others, such as PromptSmart, offer a voice-activated teleprompter that scrolls as you speak and adapts to your pace. This tool can be invaluable when you need to deliver a polished presentation without memorizing the entire script. For those looking to refine their verbal and non-verbal communication, LikeSo offers real-time feedback on your pacing and use of filler words, helping to create a smoother delivery. Integrating these apps into your preparation routine boosts your confidence and ensures that each presentation is precise, engaging, and impactful.

Transitioning to delivery, Virtual Reality (VR) technology, as was mentioned earlier in the book, is a cutting-edge tool for public speaking practice and anxiety management. VR platforms like Virtual Orator and Public Speaking VR place you in a simulated environment with an audience that reacts in real-time. This immersive experience allows you to practice your speeches in various settings, from small boardrooms to large auditoriums, providing a realistic and controlled environment where you can refine your skills. The feedback these platforms provide on aspects such as audience engagement and your use of gestures offers invaluable insights that can be difficult to gain in traditional practice settings. Moreover, for speakers who experience anxiety, practising in a VR setting can significantly reduce the fear of real-world audiences by allowing repeated exposure in a safe, controlled environment, gradually building your confidence.

Furthermore, the power of social media is understated

when discussing technological aids for public speakers. Platforms such as LinkedIn, X (formerly Twitter), and Facebook are not only venues for networking, but are also powerful tools for establishing and enhancing your speaking profile. You can create an interactive dialogue that can significantly increase your visibility and influence by sharing snippets of your presentations, engaging with your audience through posts and comments, and even live-streaming your speeches. These platforms also offer the opportunity to gather informal feedback through audience reactions and comments, providing a continuous loop of engagement that can inform and improve your future presentations. Additionally, targeting ads on these platforms can help promote your speaking events to a broader audience, ensuring higher attendance and more significant impact.

Lastly, staying abreast of emerging technology trends is crucial for maintaining relevance in the ever-evolving field of public speaking. Innovations such as augmented reality (AR) for presentations, AI-driven analytics for speech improvement, and advanced audience analytics tools are shaping the future of public speaking. By keeping informed about these developments, you can continually adapt and incorporate new technologies into your repertoire, ensuring that your speaking style remains modern, engaging, and effective. Whether it is adapting your presentations to include interactive AR elements that captivate your audience or using AI to analyze and adjust your speech patterns, the potential for growth and improvement is limitless.

As you embrace these technological tools and integrate them into your public speaking practice, you transform your presentations and your ability to connect with and impact your audience. From apps that aid in speech preparation to VR environments that enhance practice sessions and social media platforms that expand your reach and engagement, technology offers many opportunities to elevate your public speaking to new heights. Embracing these tools allows you to deliver a speech and an experience that resonates and inspires.

BEYOND THE STAGE: PUBLIC SPEAKING FOR MEDIA APPEARANCES

When you step beyond the traditional stage into the world of media appearances—television, radio, or podcasts—the dynamics of public speaking change significantly. Preparing for these appearances requires a nuanced approach, as each medium has unique challenges and expectations. For television, your visual presence is as critical as your verbal message. This medium demands high energy levels and the ability to communicate effectively through words, facial expressions, and body language. Dress appropriately for the camera, considering how colors and patterns appear on screen, and practice speaking in succinct, impactful sound bites that convey your key messages quickly and effectively. For radio, where your voice carries your entire message, focus on modulating your tone, pace, and pitch to keep listeners engaged. Podcasts, however, offer a more conversational tone and often allow for deeper dives into topics, requiring you to balance detailed content with engaging storytelling.

Maintaining message consistency across these varied media channels is crucial. Regardless of the platform, you want your core message to resonate with your audience. This consistency helps reinforce your brand and ensures that your audience receives a uniform message, whether they watch a TV interview, listen to a radio spot, or tune into a podcast. To achieve this, develop a clear, concise message that you can quickly adapt to different formats. Prepare several key points that support this message and use them as anchors in your appearances. This does not mean you cannot tailor your delivery or examples to specific audiences or formats; rather, the core of your message should remain steadfast, providing a consistent thread across all media appearances.

Handling live questions during media appearances can be particularly challenging, especially when the questions are unexpected or difficult. Effective handling of live questions shows your expertise and ability to remain composed under pressure. The key to success in these situations is preparation and presence of mind.

Before any media appearance:

i. Prepare potential questions, especially those that could put you on the spot.
ii. Think about the most challenging questions you might face and plan your responses.
iii. During the interview, listen carefully to each question, take a moment to gather your thoughts, and respond calmly and clearly. If you don't know the answer, it is okay to say so; offer to provide more information later or steer the conversation back to what you know.

Leveraging media appearances effectively can amplify your message and extend your reach. To make the most of these opportunities, view each appearance as part of a larger strategy to enhance your visibility and impact.

After each appearance:

i. Share the video or audio on your social media platforms.
  ii. Embed it on your website.
  iii. Include it in your newsletters.

This extends the life of the content and helps you reach a broader audience that may not have seen the live broadcast or streaming. Additionally, analyze the feedback and audience engagement from these shares to gauge the effectiveness of your message and delivery. This ongoing loop of presentation, feedback, and adjustment allows you to refine your approach continually, ensuring that each media appearance builds your reputation and amplifies your voice in the public domain.

Navigating the world of media appearances requires a blend of preparation, adaptability, and strategic thinking. As you gain more experience in handling these varied formats, you will discover not just how to adjust your message for different audiences and platforms but also how to use these opportunities to forge a deeper connection with your audience, expanding your influence and reinforcing your position as a trusted voice in your field. Each interview, each question, and each broadcast become a stepping stone to greater visibility and impact, harnessing the power of media to take your public speaking beyond the stage and into the lives and devices of a global audience.

CRAFTING YOUR BRAND THROUGH PUBLIC SPEAKING

In public speaking, your voice is not merely a tool for communication—it is a pivotal element in shaping and expressing your brand. A strong brand sets you apart in a crowded marketplace, establishing your reputation and credibility. You consistently present a blend of your unique skills, experiences, and personality to your audience. Each speaking engagement offers a chance to reinforce or redefine how others see you, and mastering this can significantly boost your professional trajectory.

Personal Branding Fundamentals

Building a personal brand through public speaking begins with understanding what you stand for and what you offer that is distinctively valuable. Your brand should reflect your professional expertise, values, and vision. It should resonate with your target audience, addressing their needs and aspirations. Start by clearly defining your unique selling propositions—what can you deliver that others cannot? This clarity helps you craft speeches that deliver value and consistently reinforce your brand attributes. For example, if innovation and forward-thinking are central to your brand, your presentations should regularly incorporate cutting-edge ideas and insights that reflect these qualities.

Storytelling and Brand Identity

Effective storytelling is a powerful tool for conveying your brand identity. Stories allow you to highlight your values and personality in a way that factual presentations cannot. They create emotional connections with your audience, making your message—and, by extension, your brand—more memorable. When crafting stories, focus on narratives that reflect your brand's key messages. If your brand is about overcoming challenges, share personal anecdotes about significant obstacles you have faced and how you overcame them. These stories should be authentic and align closely with the professional image you wish to project, ensuring that your brand identity is compelling and coherent.

Consistency Across Platforms

In today's digital age, your public speaking engagements are complemented by your online presence—on social media, blogs, or podcasts. It is crucial to maintain consistency across all these platforms. This consistency reinforces your brand identity and helps build trust with your audience. Ensure that the tone, style, and content of your presentations align with what you post online. If you advocate for environmental sustainability in your speeches, your social media platforms should also reflect support for sustainability initiatives. This alignment across different mediums strengthens your brand, making it more robust and recognizable.

Measuring Impact

To truly understand the effectiveness of your public speaking on your brand, you need to measure its impact. This can be done through various methods, such as audience feedback, social media engagement metrics, and professional opportunities that arise post-engagement. Tools like Google Analytics can track the increase in website traffic following your speaking events, while social media platforms provide insights into engagement rates and audience growth. Moreover, pay attention to qualitative feedback—what are people saying about you after your presentations? Are they perceiving and echoing the brand messages you intend to convey? Adjust your strategies based on these insights to fine tune the impact of your brand.

As you continue using public speaking as a platform to build and refine your brand, remember that each word you speak, each story you tell, and each message you deliver contribute to a larger narrative about who you are and what you stand for. This ongoing process enhances your immediate audience connections and solidifies your reputation in the broader professional community. With each speech, you are not just reaching out to listeners, but are inviting them into your professional world, offering them a consistent and compelling view of your unique perspectives and capabilities. Thus, effective public speaking becomes a strategic tool in your branding arsenal that can elevate your professional identity and open new avenues for growth and opportunity.

In conclusion, the strategies discussed in this chapter are integral to leveraging public speaking as a powerful mechanism for personal branding. From understanding the fundamentals of branding and employing storytelling to maintaining consistency across platforms and measuring impact, each element plays a vital role in shaping how you are perceived professionally.

CONCLUSION

As this journey reaches its conclusion, it is essential to reflect on the transformative journey you have undertaken. From the initial steps of cultivating the right mindset for public speaking to mastering the art of crafting compelling content and delivering it confidently, each chapter has built upon the last, equipping you with the skills necessary to excel in any speaking scenario. You have learned how to prepare, perform, adapt, and thrive in diverse speaking environments, from the boardroom to the stage and even in impromptu situations. Throughout this book, we have emphasized practicality—integrating exercises, real-world examples, and actionable tips tailored to enhance your public speaking prowess. These elements were designed to be read and applied, challenging you to actively engage with and implement the material in your daily interactions.

It is worth acknowledging the progress you have made. Reflect on your initial apprehensions about public speaking and measure them against the confidence you have gained through practice and persistence. Each page turned and each exercise completed has contributed to your growth as a speaker and a leader. However, the journey continues. Much like any other skill, public speaking requires continuous practice and dedication. I encourage you to keep the momentum going—seek opportunities to speak, gather feedback, and refine your approach. The landscape of communication evolves, and so should your strategies and techniques.

I invite you to share your journey of mastering public speaking with me. Connect through social media or our dedicated website to exchange experiences and insights. Your feedback is invaluable as a testament to your achievements and a cornerstone for future editions of this guide. I will writing further books and guides to help you in your journey of public speaking, but also in helping you develop further professional skills to help you excel in whichever field you are in.

Finally, remember that the art of public communication is a pathway to influence and inspire. Whether you are addressing a small team or an auditorium full of people, your voice can enact change. To echo the words of the legendary speaker Jim Rohn, "The challenge of leadership is to be strong, but not rude; be kind, but not weak; be bold, but not a bully; be thoughtful, but not lazy; be humble, but not timid; be proud, but not arrogant; have humor, but without folly."

May this book serve as your guide, your inspiration, and your steppingstone to becoming a speaker who not only speaks but speaks to make a difference. Embrace each opportunity, engage every audience, and elevate every message. Your journey to impact begins now.

DID YOU BENEFIT FROM THIS BOOK?

Public Speaking Mastery Made Simple

Congratulations! Now that you've learned all the steps to **speak with confidence, captivate your audience, and share your message with ease**, it's time to pass on your new knowledge and show others where they can find the same support.

By leaving your honest opinion of this book on Amazon, you'll help other budding speakers, professionals, and learners who want to build their skills. Your review can guide them to the tools and insights they need to share their voices with confidence, just like you.

Thank you for your support. Your feedback helps me reach

more people, empowering them to overcome stage fright and shine as speakers.

<u>Scan the QR code below to leave your review:</u>

BIBLIOGRAPHY

Rewiring the Brain to Eliminate Fear. Psychology Today. https://www.psychologytoday.com/us/blog/demystifying-psychiatry/201311/rewiring-the-brain-eliminate-fear

Why Vulnerability Will Change Your Life: The Oower of Vulnerability. BetterUp. https://www.betterup.com/blog/vulnerability

Seeing Is Believing: The Power of Visualization. Psychology Today. https://www.psychologytoday.com/us/blog/flourish/200912/seeing-is-believing-the-power-visualization

Cho, J. (2016, October 5). *Overcoming Fear of Public Speaking through Mindfulness.* Forbes. https://www.forbes.com/sites/jeenacho/2016/10/05/overcoming-fear-of-public-speaking-through-mindfulness/Author Name (n.d.). *Inside the Debate About Power Posing: A Q&A with Amy Cuddy.* Website Name. https://ideas.ted.com/inside-the-debate-about-power-posing-a-q-a-with-amy-cuddy/

Breathing Techniques for Stress Relief. WebMD. https://www.webmd.com/balance/stress-management/stress-relief-breathing-techniques

6 Most Common Rituals Before Public Speaking. https://www.sefe-mt.com/careers/blog/6-most-common-rituals-before-public-speaking/#:~:text=It%20allows%20for%20a%20calmer,to%20make%20audiences%20tune%20out

Effects of Exercise and Physical Activity on Anxiety. PubMed Central. https://www.ncbi.nlm.nih.gov/pmc/articles/PMC3632802/

Structuring the Speech. Department of Communication, University of Pittsburgh https://www.comm.pitt.edu/structuring-speech

Audience Analysis – Public Speaking. Open Maricopa https://open.maricopa.edu/com225/chapter/need-to-find-audience-analysis-reading/

Speech Introductions. https://www.unr.edu/writing-speaking-center/writing-speaking-resources/speech-introductions

Powerful Storytelling for Public Speakers. https://projectcharisma.com/storytelling-for-public-speakers-guide/

Quick Easy Effective Tips for Vocal Variety in Speech: 14 Exercises. https://www.write-out-loud.com/quickeasyeffectivetipsforvocalvariety.html

Author Name. (n.d.). *Speech Pauses: 12 Techniques to Speak Volumes with Your Silence.* https://sixminutes.dlugan.com/pause-speech/

How Positive Body Language Improves Your Public Speaking. https://www.

entrepreneur.com/leadership/how-positive-body-language-improves-your-public-speaking/452296

How to Use Humor Effectively in Speeches: 6 Tips with Examples. https://www.write-out-loud.com/how-to-use-humor-effectively.html

6 Best Persuasion Techniques That You Can Use in Your Speeches. SpeakerHub https://speakerhub.com/skillcamp/6-best-persuasion-techniques-you-can-use-your-speeches

Harnessing the Power of Rhetorical Questions in Speeches. LinkedIn. https://www.linkedin.com/pulse/harnessing-power-rhetorical-questions-speeches-jagatheswaran-mib-w7nkc

Storytelling Techniques for Presentations [Real Case Study]. Maurizio La Cava https://www.mauriziolacava.com/en/storytelling-techniques-for-presentations-real-case-study/

Handling the Q&A Session – 8 Public Speaking Tools. https://craigvalentine.com/handling-qa-session-8-public-speaking-tools/

The 4 Design Principles in PowerPoint. https://www.presentationload.com/blog/the-4-design-principles-in-powerpoint/

Make Your Presentations Memorable Using Props. SketchBubble https://www.sketchbubble.com/blog/make-your-presentations-memorable-using-props/

15 Strategies for Engaging Virtual Presentations. https://lars-sudmann.com/15-strategies-for-engaging-virtual-presentations/

The 6 Best Live Polling Tools to Engage Your Audience. https://slideswith.com/blog/best-live-polling-tools

How to Create an Elevator Pitch with Examples. https://careerservices.fas.harvard.edu/blog/2022/10/11/how-to-create-an-elevator-pitch-with-examples/

Dearnell, A. (2023, February 22). *7 Golden Rules for Successful Panel Discussions.* Forbes. https://www.forbes.com/sites/adriandearnell/2023/02/22/7-golden-rules-for-successful-panel-discussions/

How to Present an Engaging Keynote Speech. https://iccbelfast.com/blogs/presenting-keynote-speech#:~:text=Rachael's%20top%20tips%20when%20deciding,and%20leaves%20a%20lasting%20impression

Workshop Facilitation Techniques for Exceptional Results. https://www.skillpacks.com/facilitation-techniques/

How to Give Effective Feedback (The Toastmasters Guide). CareerFair. https://www.careerfair.io/reviews/toastmasters-effective-feedback

Best Tools and Methods for Public Speaking Skills Assessment. Linkedin. https://www.linkedin.com/advice/1/what-some-best-tools-methods-self-

assessment-public#:~:text=A%20rubric%20is%20a%20-
tool,%2C%20language%2C%20and%20audience%20engagement
Why Toastmasters? Website Name. https://www.toastmasters.org/member ship/why-toastmasters#:~:text=You'll%20improve%20your%20interper-sonal,your%20personal%20and%20professional%20goals
10 Emerging Trends Every Speaker Should Know. https://publicspeakingacad emy.co.uk/the-future-of-public-speaking-10-emerging-trends-every-speaker-should-know/
Cherry, K. (2022, December 7). *What is the Spotlight Effect?* Verywell Mind. https://www.verywellmind.com/what-is-the-spotlight-effect-3024470
Gilovich, T., Medvec, V. H., & Savitsky, K. (2000). *The Spotlight Effect in Social Judgment: An Egocentric Bias in Estimates of the Salience of One's Own Actions and Appearance.* Journal of Personality and Social Psychology, 78(2), 211-222. https://doi.org/10.1037/0022-3514.78.2.211